GROWING INTO FREEDOM

GROWING INTO FREEDOM
A Way to Make Sense of Ourselves

Edward Moss

eagle

Copyright © 1993 Edward Moss

British Library Cataloguing-in-Publication Data. A catalogue record for
this book is available from the British Library

Published by Eagle, an imprint of Inter Publishing Service (IPS) Ltd,
59 Woodbridge Road, Guildford Surrey GU1 4RF.

All Scripture quotations, unless otherwise noted, are taken from the
Holy Bible,
Revised Standard Version.

Typeset by The Electronic Book Factory Ltd, Fife, Scotland.
Printed in the UK by HarperCollins Manufacturing, Glasgow.

ISBN No: 0 86347 074 2

CONTENTS

Chapter Five: LOVING AND BEING LOVED

FOREWORD

Four years ago, Edward Moss published *Seeing Man Whole*, a magisterial and highly original essay on the foundations of therapeutic practice in psychology. Central to this major work was the idea that we could have no useful or intelligible 'healing art' in psychotherapy, any more than in other areas, without a controlling vision of what the self might be – a sort of ideal story of the self as a growing and unified system. This may sound uncontroversial enough or commonsensical enough, but it is far from an easy or obvious position to defend in modern psychology or philosophy.

What it assumes is that our reflection on ourselves, especially in the context of the decisions we make, has built into it a picture of the self that is possible and desirable for us – what is described in the present work as the 'anticipating self'. In this perspective, we recognise that we can't properly think of ourselves as timeless or fixed entities: knowing ourselves is knowing our histories *and* knowing the kind of history that might unfold from where we now are. No analysis of competing forces can replace an awareness of the stories we tell ourselves about ourselves – and which we also communicate in a host of diverse ways to those we relate to.

So what we have here is a thoroughly practical and splendidly readable application of these general principles to the task of *making* as well as *seeing* ourselves whole. The great classics of theory, from Jung to Winnicott, are deployed expertly and critically in charting the course of intelligible human development and the risks and wounds that may beset this process. At every point, Dr Moss draws on a wide range of non-technical material for illumination; we meet here Shakespeare and George Herbert alongside the founding scriptures of psychiatry, and also a sensitive and searching use of case studies. Notably and boldly, Dr Moss also brings into play the themes and narratives of Christian faith, in a way that both gives depth to his therapeutic discussions and gives new concreteness and clarity to familiar Christian notions, bringing the language of the New Testament alive in all sorts of unexpected dimensions. I was especially grateful for the insights on sin, grace and addiction in the fourth chapter, and found myself constantly challenged and educated by these crisp and vivid pages.

This book is unmistakeably a professional's work – a professional in both the theory and the practice of mending souls; but it is accessible to any receptive reader, economical, clear and patient in its exposition. It will be a precious resource for the pastor or counsellor (for the good physician as well, I think), but can also be read with enormous profit by anyone who simply wants to enlarge his or her understanding of the human task.

† Rowan Williams

INTRODUCTION

This book has grown out of experience in the counselling room. Its purpose is to give an account of human nature, and of the ways in which human beings can move towards healing and freedom. The system I have followed has been to suggest a series of frames of understanding intended to help us to make sense of different aspects of ourselves. It is a book about interpretations and understandings, not about the process and techniques of counselling, on which it touches only incidentally and indirectly.

As a counsellor, after I have listened carefully to a client's story and we have talked about the problems that arise, I may try, when the moment seems appropriate, to offer some tentative interpretation of what has been going on for him or her. If this clicks and seems right to the client we can build upon it; but if not we either modify it together in discussion or we drop it. 'An interpretation that does not work', as D.W. Winnicott put it, 'always means that I have made the interpretation at the wrong moment or in the wrong way and I withdraw it unconditionally.'[1] (It could also be the wrong interpretation altogether.) In another characteristic sentence Winnicott says: 'I think I interpret mainly to let the patient know the limits of my understanding.'[2] Within the narrower scope of counselling, as distinct from psychotherapy, I think I try to do the same.

However if you have no general frame of reference it is often difficult to grasp and express what is going on in you. I therefore often find myself first offering clients a general account of some aspect of human nature, within which they may find it easier to place and describe their own experience. This may come at a fairly early stage, before we begin to try out any specific interpretation of the client's own situation. To offer such an account is to provide a sort of picture or metaphor that defines – if the client can accept it – a space within which we can usefully work together. Over the years I find that I have collected, without particularly intending to, a repertoire of these accounts, which build up between them a more or less coherent picture of many aspects of human psychology.

It is by putting these accounts together and elaborating them that I have constructed this book. They have been expanded in some cases a long way beyond the improvisations of the counselling room, but they still retain the character of sketches, metaphorical frames through which it may be possible to grasp something of the uniqueness of individual lives. They are meant to be suggestive, rather than comprehensive or authoritative; they are to be used if they are helpful, discarded if they are not. My hope is that in a similar way this book will prove useful to people who want to come to deeper self-knowledge, creating a space of their own within which they can recognize and place themselves.

I have drawn my theoretical ideas on human psychology from a variety of sources, including some work of my own. When appropriate, I have referred to these sources, but in a simple book I have tried to keep notes to a minimum. What is relatively unusual, however, and I think important, is that I have drawn frequently on ideas from the Bible. I believe the New Testament account of human nature is profoundly true; and this understanding provides the matrix in which my scattered insights are held together. I do not feel myself to be merely relating Christian understandings to the world of modern psychology, translating Christianity into psychological terms. Rather I feel that I am bringing the insights of psychology to help me to a better and deeper understanding of some aspects of the gospel itself. I do not find myself trying to resolve conflicts between two perspectives on the truth. On the contrary I find that for me it is only within the wider and deeper perspective of New Testament teaching about love, grace, forgiveness, healing and freedom that what I have learned of the academic and clinical science of psychology comes to full coherence and clarity.

At the same time I would emphasise that while this book draws happily and unashamedly upon the resources of the New Testament, it does not preach, or try to press Christian views on the reader. Many of my clients are not Christians and the book is intended to be accessible and helpful to people of any faith or none.

Where case material is used, all names have been changed and other details fictionalized. In all such cases a great deal is left out. These stories are to be seen as diagrammatic illustrations based on experience, not as portraits of actual people.

I owe a special debt of gratitude to my clients, without whose help and testing the material for this book would never have been produced. I am also much indebted to my colleagues of the Emmaus Counselling Service, and to our supervisor Mrs. Marjorie Hudson. I, should like, further, to express particular thanks to Robin Hodgkin, Roger Hurding and Christopher Holland, who read the book in draft and made many extremely helpful suggestions. The responsibility for faults and errors, however, is entirely mine.

Edward Moss

CHAPTER ONE

I WANT TO BE ME: CHILDHOOD AND ADOLESCENCE

Being True to Ourselves

Every human life is a journey of self-discovery, never quite completed. It is a journey of continual venturings. I find myself (if I am blessed with good enough parents) in a place where I am safe, secure and loved; so I have the courage to venture out. I encounter the reality of the world beyond. I respond to reality, and in the process I express and so discover myself. Then I find myself in a new place where I have to draw on new strength and establish a new security. From there once more I venture into life, to express and renew myself again. It is in responding to reality, in deciding and acting, that we discover and create ourselves.

In each new situation, as we respond, we present a new face to the world. A new aspect of ourselves is revealed, which may include facets never previously brought into being. We are not ordinarily aware of our responding selves, but when we look back, or when we are deliberately self-conscious, we can become aware of these 'faces'. I can look back on myself yesterday, when I happened to be so angry, and what I see is someone quite different from the person I am today.

Each of these faces of myself represents me in the given situation. It stands for me. Yet it is not the whole of me. The whole of me is something far greater, something which includes all my past experience, all my thoughts

and feelings, my memories, my fears and hopes and
dreams. It cannot possibly be grasped as a whole in
consciousness; I can only grasp, at any one time, one face
which stands for me. The real me is not a transparent
ghost, or a selection of memories or dispositions, which
can be subtracted from the whole. Nor can I effectively
be divided into a mind bit and a body bit. To think about
me I have to think of the whole me. It is the continuity of
the whole which defines me.[1] And it is this whole which
grows, in a sort of continuous creation, throughout my
life, as my temporary selves decide and act in their
encounter with the world, representing me and adding
to me, for better or for worse. It is this whole which, to
use St. Paul's great image, is sown at the end of my life,
a perishable, natural body, and then, as I believe, raised
imperishable, in total transformation, beyond all mortal
comprehension, a spiritual body.[2]

In the previous paragraph I have outlined in the
broadest terms a general theory of the self. It is inevitably
not beyond controversy, since there is no theory today
which is generally accepted. But it includes at least some
aspects of the truth, and I would ask the reader to accept
it for the time being as a working assumption that defines
what I am trying to talk about.

Often, looking back, I am dissatisfied with what my
temporary selves have done. To quote St. Paul again, 'I
do not even acknowledge my own actions as mine, for
what I do is not what I want to do, but what I detest.'[3]
Yet the trouble is not really that I fail to obey moral rules.
The trouble with my temporary selves is that they have
not been authentic. They have not been spontaneous,
fearless, naturally creative, with the creativity of the
Spirit of life within me. They have not been free and
genuine in reflecting the hidden self. Somehow they have
not represented the real me.

But then, what right have I to feel that the real me is
any different from what I have actually done and been?
I do indeed have that feeling; but then I also have the

feeling that I am responsible for what I have done with my life; that too is me, and I cannot escape from it. To cut the answer short, I believe the truth is that we are all made in the image and likeness of God; we all have the potential to share in his creativity, in the perfect freedom which is obedience to his will; but we are flawed, fallen creatures, and rather than being set free by obedience to the Spirit of the whole, we find ourselves constantly in bondage to the compulsions of the part. Indeed often we have no awareness of what such a free obedience would mean. We don't know who we are.

How this happens we shall consider more closely in a later chapter. For the present it is sufficient to say that it is entirely legitimate to cry out, as so many people do, 'I want to be *me*'.

> This above all, – to thine own self be true;
> And it must follow, as the night the day,
> Thou canst not then be false to any man.[4]

This advice which Polonius gave to Laertes has real meaning. There is a hidden, buried self – what is called in the first epistle of Peter 'the hidden person of the heart' – to which our temporary selves in their daily dealing with the world can be true and can be false. It is right to seek to be true; and it is never too late to try. The grace is always there and it is always possible to be set free.

In pursuing this theme our first task must be to consider how these temporary selves come into being and so create, day by day, our track through time and space. I have suggested that it is essentially by venturing and responding that we discover ourselves. Although the process is unceasing, it is possible to identify a number of stages through which we all pass in our lives, at which the venturing and responding have to take a certain kind of shape; and it is also possible to recognize certain patterns of failure at each of these stages which, if they are not overcome, can lead to

further trouble later in life. In the sections that follow
I consider these stages one by one, using broadly the
demarcations which Erik Erikson has made familiar in
his well-known book *Childhood and Society*.[5] My aim is
not to attempt any comprehensive account, but rather to
offer for each stage a brief sketch of possibilities, a frame
within which the details and idiosyncrasies of particular
cases can be placed and understood.

Venturing Out: (1) The Baby

The first crucial event is that of birth itself, very much
a venture into the world, and one in which the baby
participates as well as the mother. There is a good
deal of evidence to suggest that if a baby is unwanted
or resented, or if the mother herself is ill or miserable or
insecure during the pregnancy or the birth, this can make
the process more of an exhausting ordeal, less of a joyful
venture; and such an experience can cast its shadow into
the future. Once born, the baby has an immediate need to
be loved and held and made to feel secure. It is important
that a close bond should be established early with the
mother. At every stage in life it is love which creates
and affirms a person's sense of identity, and with it the
confidence to venture and to live and grow.

During the first year and more of a child's life, when
it is still totally dependent on the mother, its identity is
closely bound up with the mother's, and there is little
awareness of boundaries between self and not-self. There
are needs to be met for feeding, for sleep, for holding
and security and play, and it is only gradually that the
baby comes to recognize those who meet these needs as
separate persons. Only gradually, through venturing, as
the power to know and control its own movements, and to
recognize and reach for the things around it is developed,
can the baby begin to have a sense of itself as bounded
in space and possessing definite capacities rather than a
sort of indefinite omnipotence.

This stage is particularly important for establishing what Erikson calls 'basic trust' (the equivalent of what Laing calls 'ontological security',[6] and Lake calls 'acceptance'[7]). This grows from the 'holding environment', and failure or weakness over establishing it in early childhood can lead to difficulties over finding the necessary trust to cope confidently with the world in later life. Not that a perfect environment is needed. Growing up involves learning to cope with the imperfections of the world, and for the baby this includes coping with occasional frustrations and the uncontrollable absences of those who attend it. But any failure of 'good enough' mothering, to use Winnicott's phrase, can leave a lasting trace. And if there is prolonged failure, or there are many such failures, an emotional pattern may be established which can be set off again in later life, with serious consequences, by any episode of apparent rejection.

If a baby is separated for a long time from its mother, according to Frank Lake's analysis (and many other accounts are very similar), it feels an increasing separation anxiety, which may grow into terror, dread and despair; and in reaction it may develop fantasies of aggression accompanied by rage, or else fantasies of the mother's return. These are essentially ways of trying to cope with the stress, they are defences against the ultimate threat of disintegration. When mother does return they will fade into the past; but if the experience was intense and prolonged enough, these defensive patterns, with their accompanying emotions of rage, or desire, or terror, or dread, or despair, can be brought irrationally to life again by events that occur many years later; and in this way they can distort our capacity as adults to respond with simplicity and realism to the challenges of today.

Where basic trust has not been well established in infancy, one consequence in later years can be an excessive dependence on support from others — sometimes translated into a dependence on food or alcohol. Another

consequence can be some form of withdrawal, or retreat
into a fantasy world. Again, when a baby has not successfully grown through the stage of establishing boundaries
between self and not-self, the result can be a 'narcissistic' type of personality. Narcissists may seem to be
preoccupied with images of themselves in fluctuating,
sometimes grandiose roles, but in fact this preoccupation
with self covers a deep-lying uncertainty about their
very identity. We all need the security of being loved
and valued if we are to love and value ourselves, and
so have the confidence to venture out effectively in our
lives. And this in turn is necessary if we are to be able
to give ourselves in love to other people.

Another possibility, where basic trust has not been
well established, is the tendency, analysed by Melanie
Klein, to separate too much pictures of the good mother
from the bad, and thereafter to see the world in terms
of idealized, angelic figures and persecuting, demonic
figures, on whom all the unsatisfactoriness of life can
be projected. A further possibility seems to be associated
with the baby's sense of omnipotence. This is the fear
that its own rage and aggression may have destroyed or
driven away the good mother, a fear that can lead to a
deep-seated, irrational sense of guilt and worthlessness.

I have suggested that it is in the encounter with reality
that we discover ourselves; and it follows that when we
fail to cope with reality and begin to escape from the
truth, our inner selves begin to be twisted and distorted.
But, as T.S. Eliot said, human kind cannot bear very
much reality. We have to learn step by step, in childhood
and throughout our lives, within what Winnicott called
'the *potential space* between the individual and the
environment',[8] to cope creatively with more and more
of the reality of the world. Truth itself is the healer;
but too much at once will overwhelm us, and we have
to learn to cope with a little at a time. Through the
stages of growth and maturity we gradually build up
our capacity 'to see life steadily and see it whole'. But

if our passage through one of the earlier stages has not been fully successful, there will remain an unfinished process of growing into truth to be completed; and it is the function of counselling or psychotherapy to provide a framework of concerned attention, love and support, within which the individual is enabled to complete this bit of growing up.

Venturing Out (2): The Toddler

As a child learns to crawl, and then to stand and toddle and run, we see vividly how she is encouraged to venture out from mother's knee to discover a new world and new capabilities; how much pleasure these achievements give her (and her parents too); how, when things go wrong and she falls over something, she totters back with tears to mother, to be comforted and loved, and encouraged to venture out once more. In this way she tries out a new independence and discovers more of herself.

This is a time of rapidly growing physical achievement, not only in movement but in dexterity of hand and limb, and in control of the movements of bowels and bladder. It is also the time when a child begins to understand and to use words. As Michael Jacobs has written, 'Properly negotiated, this stage lays the foundation of self-esteem and pride in achievement, together with the pleasure of self-expression. Negotiated less well, this stage sows the seeds of doubt, shame and inhibition.'[9]

This is a time when the boundaries between self and mother become much more sharply defined, as the sense of an independent self develops. There is a clearer opposition, and sometimes conflict, between self and others. Parental attitudes to the child's new achievements – whether the parents are easy-going or pressing, interested or distracted, encouraging or threatening – can have a lasting effect on the child's own future attitudes, particularly in regard to authority. A stifling, controlling regime can be reflected later in a rigid, fearful attitude to authority, a stickling for details, and a constant fear of letting things get out of control, which is sometimes expressed in obsessional rituals. But much depends on the child. Where one child might react in that way, another might react towards a rebellious anarchism; and this too can be an unsatisfactory foundation for the future.

The struggle and achievement of toilet training plays an important part, not least in the development of a sense of shame over any failure of control, any falling short of our own high standards. As this suggests, the toddler stage is one in which the ideas and standards of the parents tend to be adopted as part of the child's own self, reflecting the formation of what Freud called the over-I, or super-ego. This is a kind of composite, judgemental parent-figure within the child, who rewards and punishes, praises and condemns whatever the child is doing. Gradually this super-ego is incorporated into the self and the direct link with the parents sinks out of consciousness. But the super-ego which we adopt or create in childhood, whether loving, consistent and relaxed, or harsh, arbitrary and frightening, always remains with us and has an important influence across our lives on the way in which we cope with reality and express our temporary selves.

A significant by-product of the establishment of the super-ego is that it makes possible a sense of 'righteous' anger or aggression. When a very young child expresses anger or aggression, it will almost inevitably be directed against the parent figures, and will therefore be disapproved by them. With the formation of the super-ego, internalized parent figures are established who can encourage and justify angry or aggressive behaviour, even if it is directed against the true parents; and this is important in enabling a child to have the strength to stand up for itself and so to become an independent personality.

The super-ego has an important function as a sort of

inbuilt gyroscope or automatic pilot, which can always provide an instant judgment, an instant steer through the moral undergrowth of our lives. Without it we would have to work every decision out from first principles and life is too short for such a process. But conversely a person whose decisions are always dominated by an unconscious automatic pilot with childishly simplistic ideas is liable to run into trouble in the real world and to be intolerably difficult for other people to deal with. We need the strength and liberating discipline of the super-ego, but it is important for the conscious self to be in charge, in touch with the super-ego but also in control of it.

According to the concepts of 'Transactional Analysis'[10] we can recognize in every grown person a Parent, an Adult and a Child. We need all three. The object of therapy in this perspective is, first, to ensure that the three are clearly distinguished, so that there is neither 'contamination' of the Adult by Parent or Child, nor 'blocking out' of either Parent or Child; and, secondly, to ensure that the Adult remains both in touch with the others and ultimately in charge of what happens. For it is the Adult who is in direct contact with reality today and calculates rationally the consequences of the actions that are taken. Transactional Analysis is not sufficient, in my view, as a general account of human psychology, but in its own broad terms it carries a lot of force, particularly where the analysis of relationships is concerned. Its roots clearly lie primarily in the toddler stage and the small child stage that follows.

There are many ways in which a child can encounter difficulties in the toddler stage that can have lasting effects. If the parent's approval is endlessly made conditional on success in performing some task, this can seriously undermine the basic trust which is always needed if we are to venture out with confidence. We need to be loved first for our own sake, for what we are, before being affirmed for what we do. If the parents' behaviour is contradictory and sends conflicting messages, the super-ego in later years can be capriciously inconsistent, and the grown person can become uncertain of identity and confused in purpose. The toddler is constantly doing new things, but in the process she inevitably runs into new hurts and frustrations. She can find herself swept by torrential emotions and frightened of losing control in a way which may stir something of the deeper-lying rages and terrors of babyhood. She still needs the security of being firmly held, not only physically when she runs back to mother or father, but also in the wider sense of knowing that even if she loses control her outbursts will be safely contained. This can be a time in which tantrums may break out, which are a testing of the surrounding barriers and a testing of the parents' love. Not to be held, not to be stopped, not to find any limits and barriers can be much more alarming and disorientating than to encounter a firm boundary when security is needed.

Venturing Out (3): The Small Child

There are of course no sharp demarcations between the stages of growth. Not only do different children pass through the same stage in different ways and at varying ages, but a child will often go back, under stress, to a pattern of behaviour characteristic of an earlier stage. What can be taken to mark most clearly the difference between the toddler stage and that of the small child is a more acute awareness of other people, and in particular the parents, as separate persons with whom individual relationships are developed. With this comes an awareness of sexual identity on both sides of the relationship, an interest in sexual differences, and some beginnings of sexual curiosity and pleasure in the stimulation of the genitals. Psychoanalysts identify this as the genital stage, as compared with the anal stage preceding it; in the oral stage of babyhood before that the pleasures and frustrations of feeding and the process of exploration by 'suck it and see' were predominant.

In this stage the child becomes concerned not only with venturing away from mother (in constant awareness of her presence near by as a safe refuge), but also with finding in father no longer just an assistant to mother, but a strong friend who will take the child's hand and help her to explore; not only that, a father who assures and protects the safe place which is home for all three. Now there is a triangular relationship; and the child becomes one who not only receives love but gives love. There is a whole new complex of emotional possibilities. Feelings of rivalry and envy may emerge; and where there are brothers and sisters the cross-currents of emotion become all the more confusing.

This is the stage which Freud associated with the myth of Oedipus who, all unknowing, murdered his father and married his mother. It certainly does not follow that every little boy literally wants to murder his father and marry his mother, and every little girl the converse. But it is a necessary part of normal development to go through feelings of rivalry with the parent of the same sex and desire for exclusive possession of the parent of the opposite sex, as well as of love for each of them. It is through these experiences that we learn to know both the force of the emotions involved in close relationships, and also how they can be balanced and controlled, how boundaries can and must be set. It has been said that refusal to face the Oedipal is the principal characteristic of the narcissist, the person who cannot get away from the unboundedness and indefinite identity of babyhood and, in order to preserve it, takes refuge in illusion and false self-images. However if all goes well in this stage we begin to establish our own self by identifying with the parent of the same sex. This is the stage in which, as part of our exploration of reality, we learn our fundamental ways of managing relationships. Correspondingly it is a stage at which we can acquire destructive patterns of coping which continue to tangle up our relationships in the future.

Characteristically we learn some of these patterns from the ways in which our parents behave, not only towards us, but towards each other. Some of the most destructive effects arise when a parent oversteps the boundary of intimacy with the child, or when a parent rejects the child's need for love, or when parents try to involve the child in their own battles. Characteristically it is at this stage that we lay some, at least, of the foundations of our sexual identity, coming to terms with the fact that we can love both parents, but each in a different way – and perhaps (more or less unconsciously) with the fact that there is in each of us an element of the opposite sex which needs to be integrated as part of the completeness of the whole person.

It is not surprising that many of the problems which cause people to come for counselling have their roots in the Oedipal stage of development. These are two examples:

George had a father who was cold, critical and uninterested, a mother who was warm and loving, but herself timid and under the father's domination. He also had a brother two years older and one, much younger, sister. His mother provided him with a loving refuge, but little encouragement to venture out. His brother was jealous of the attention George kept getting from his mother, and when George tried to venture out, the brother would take every opportunity to outdo him and put him down. George generally submitted and retreated, but if driven to the limit he would go into a frantic tantrum, which would usually bring the oppression to an end; he could then go back to his mother.

In later life the brother became a highly successful businessman, married and with a family. He was not unkind to George, who discovered, to his surprise, that his brother had resented the father as much as he had. George himself, however, never having

developed, in his venturing, any firm identity or real
sticking power, tried a succession of jobs, only to give
them up as soon as any difficulty arose, especially
when he had to deal with others in authority (an
area in which his distant, fearful and resentful
relationship with his father had clearly left its
mark). He remained dependent on his mother's
comfort till she died. He worked sporadically but
acquired few qualifications. He had a number of
girlfriends but the relationships dragged themselves
out and died. In his late thirties he found himself
obsessively in love with a woman with whom he had
lived but who had decided to break the relationship
– partly because of her own problems, but mainly
because George, though a big, husky-looking man,
could offer little real strength or support, and was
constantly looking for a mother's sympathy, often
with tears and rages. In effect, it would seem, George
had missed out on an important step of development
and this had brought him great unhappiness; he still
needed to complete his growing up.

James was unwanted by his mother, who was a
dominating, vituperative woman, liable to violence.
His father was subservient and provided no firm
control. He had a tendency to buy love from the child.
James hated his mother and did not respect his
father. As he grew up, he was by turns insecure and
self-assertive. In adolescence and young manhood he
made a good start not only in his work as a bank
clerk, but also in his early relationships with girls,
and as a leader both on the football field and in the
band in which he played. But there was an underlying sense (which came out in the songs he wrote)
that he was always acting a part, trying to prove
things, living up to an image. He was reluctant to
affirm others, perhaps through a jealous insecurity.
Under stress he tended to revert to childish patterns

– withdrawing in fear, or breaking out in tantrums, shaking, tears, and actual violence (for example, towards his girlfriend or his father). He lived for some years with a girl younger than himself, whom he tended to dominate. Eventually, after a traumatic episode of jealousy and violence, she left him. James was shattered, suicidal, desperate to win her back. But she had grown away from his domination. There was no prospect of winning her back, or of building a good relationship with any other girl, till James could begin to understand his own behaviour and grow into a new maturity. It is plausible to see in his insecurity and his tendency towards narcissism a lack of basic trust rooted in the experience of a baby unwanted by his mother; and similarly to see in his behaviour under stress a small child unable to find a clear identity or effectively to recognize boundaries. In love he tended to be either dominant, possessive and jealous (so making the other person part of himself) or else dependent, servile, and trying to buy affection (so making himself part of the other).

These years of small-childhood are years in which the child acquires a vast amount of new knowledge and new skills, especially in the use of language. Children also get to know other children and a range of adults besides their parents. A great deal of learning and maturing takes place through the agency of play, especially playing with other children. Stories and picture-books become important. So far as the managing of relationships and the establishing of identity are concerned, games of the 'let's pretend' type, in which children play, for example, doctors and nurses, or fathers and mothers, can help them in their exploration of themselves and others, of pleasure, disappointment and anger, of roles and boundaries and confrontations.

In adult life it is important to be able to stay in touch with the child within. The sheer capacity of the

confident child to have fun, to be absorbed in play, to
live spontaneously in the present is sometimes lost in
the adult, and the loss is serious, particularly perhaps
where the natural enjoyment of sex is concerned. On
the other hand the child may be addicted to patterns
of behaviour which can do a lot of damage if they are
carried unconsciously into adult life, particularly when
they are used as ways of escaping from an adult response
to difficulty. Some examples might be the attempt to
manipulate others through wheedling, or self-pitying
tears, or childish rages and violence. While it is important
not to suppress the child within us, it is also important
for us not to become unconscious agents of our childish
impulses acting themselves out inappropriately in the
adult world. We need to know ourselves and to be aware
of what we are doing.

Venturing Out (4): The Schoolchild

The next stage of growth is that in which the child
ventures out for the first time on its own, beyond the
home circle into a different environment where parents
are not present, and where other children, the 'peer
group', represent the chief reality to be encountered.
Typically this happens when the child goes to school for
the first time. This is not to deny that relationships with
other children cannot be of great importance at an earlier
age; but what marks this stage out is the encounter with
the peer group outside the home, as distinct from being
with other children in some form of home environment.

In the encounter with reality we discover ourselves;
and perhaps the first thing the child discovers in this
environment is how much the peer group matters, how
desperately he or she wants to belong, how important
it is to conform, how different the ideas and values and
current fads and fashions of the group are, and how
they set home values in a different light. This inevitably
creates a conflict, which is resolved to some extent by

keeping the two worlds of home and school apart. (Some of us can well remember times when we felt embarrassed about our parents, if they appeared at school, because they did not happen to fit the stereotypes which the peer group admired.) But in many circumstances the encounter with school reality can be intimidating and often it can lead to a desire to run back to the safety of home. It is important that this security should remain available, and not be cut off too brutally; but it is also important that the child should gather the courage to go out and survive independently in the new environment.

The peer group can be cruel. It is usually at this stage that the child encounters for the first time the institution of the boss and gang, with its pecking order. This is the most basic pattern of human social structure beyond the family (as indeed of the social structure of many animal species). It is normally contained within a wider structure, that of civilization, of law and order; but it is striking in human history how, when the ordered government of civilization begins to break down for any reason, the boss and gang structure, which can be studied in prototypical form in every school playground, is likely to take over again. The boss will have his henchmen and his sycophants, his accepted followers, and finally his hangers-on or postulants, who are the slaves and butts of the rest. The whole is organized in a restless, uncomfortable way through a pecking order, established by claims, challenges and duels, and constantly changing in smaller or greater ways. The boss himself may be challenged, slaves may be accepted as followers, forces may be lost to rival gangs (and there will always be rival gangs, in potentiality if not in actuality). Meanwhile the identity of the gang is established and maintained by its own language, symbols and rituals.

The school playground version of all this is usually rudimentary rather than fully developed, and it is preserved from setting hard because children are always growing up and moving on. But in essentials it is there, and in essentials every child has to learn to recognize and cope with it, not only as an external reality, but also as part of his or her own inner reality. For we are all so constituted as to respond to this pattern; we are all both competitive and conformist, potential leaders and potential followers, potentially loyal and potential betrayers, potentially caring and potentially cruel. In the playground we learn many things about ourselves which need to be learnt; and if for any reason we miss out on this sometimes painful part of our education, we miss out on an essential part of our growing up.

The element of law and order, of authority and government, is also present in the school environment and is scarcely less important. It is again part of external reality and we have to learn to respond to it. Here the personalities of teachers and the rules and atmosphere of the regime can deeply affect our response, in what is a major step of accommodation to the world we live in. So too can the perception of authority and the pattern of response to authority already developed earlier in our lives, so too the dominant attitudes of the peer group. Generally among the peer group it is the defiant rebel and anarchist who attracts admiration, not the obedient conformist; and up to a point this is healthy; for if we are to venture out and discover ourselves effectively (and this includes discovering our own capacity for leadership), we need to encounter, challenge and test out the meaning of things in our own experience, not merely through a meek acceptance of the authority of others. Yet, on the other hand, it is necessary and even reassuring to learn the limits of defiance, to know that the security of firm government is still there.

This is a time in which the child learns a vast amount about the world beyond the home, not merely from teachers but from books and stories and television, from other children and from actual experience. Play continues to be important and much of the learning is the almost indefinable accumulation of worldly wisdom which comes

from innumerable dealings with other people of all kinds
and ages. Sexuality plays its part in the self-images
which the child may adopt in imagination. It is also
constantly present in jokes and sniggerings; and in the
modern world it is inescapable on the television and in
every manifestation of the media. Yet for children this
stage, known as the latency period, is one in which sexual
development marks time physically for a few years, boys
and girls tend to run in separate groups, and sex does not
loom so large as when puberty arrives. This is essentially
a time in which, free from the additional pressures of adolescent and adult sexual drives, and ideally without being
cut off from the secure haven of home, the child learns the
discipline of work in an organized environment, together
with a wide variety of physical, mental and social skills –
ways of coping with the world. And this is done within a
school microcosm, which is itself a kind of potential space,
intermediate between home and the hard realities of the
adult world. Children begin to discover their individual
strengths and weaknesses, to develop their individual
wants, fears and ambitions, to adopt more consciously
an individual self-image, and to know the pride of living
up to it, the shame of failing to do so.

Part of the price of this venturing out into a new world
is a tendency to separate the new self from the old, the
school persona from the home persona. Up to a point this
may be necessary, but if it goes too far it can mean a
cutting of the links to young childhood and a repressing
of the emotions associated with earlier stages of life. It
is necessary to develop at this stage a degree of sturdy
independence and something of the stiff upper lip. But
there can be lasting harm if the child, in creating a new
persona to match the expectations and compulsions of a
different world – indeed in learning to be able to put on
a necessary act – loses some of the roots of authenticity.
Especially if the transition is abrupt, as when a child is
sent to a boarding-school at an early age, there may well
be a tendency to create a sort of shell round the inner

personality. This shell becomes the outward personality of the child, while the inner, more sensitive side finds no expression, is not encouraged or developed, and gradually disappears from consciousness. This can produce in later years an adult who is rigid in conforming to an image, rather than spontaneous in expressing his or her true self, one who finds it hard to be in touch with his or her emotions, one who is afraid of losing control and whose emotional life is in some degree undeveloped and immature.

Venturing Out (5): The Teenager

With the coming of adolescence, physical growth is speeded up and sexual capability soon follows. No longer a child, but not yet an adult, the young person is venturing out from the comparatively protected world of the latency period, in which ideas and values come from the peer group or from adults in authority, and most decisions that matter are taken by others. Any generalizations about this period must be stretched over a wide range of variation, not only in what happens with each individual but also in the age at which it happens. A central feature, however, is the emergence of a more individual person, often self-conscious, uncertain and diffident, yet with a need for self-discovery and self-assertion. Swings of mood are characteristic, and this unpredictable, shifting personality can be awkward to handle, both for the teenager and for others. A degree of self-absorption is understandable as young people come to terms with the transformations of sexual maturity and with the powerful need to be noticed and respected as people with rights and opinions and wills of their own.

The young child tends to identify with a parent-figure of the same sex; and the child's basic identifications, whatever they are, do not disappear altogether; but in the teenage years they tend to be submerged. The adolescent will usually be defining his or her individuality *over*

against the parents, as part of the process of growing into
independence from them. There is a need to break free
and rebel, to occupy one's own territory. This is reflected
in the adoption of models, whether among older adolescents or teachers or sports heroes or media personalities
or others, who may be incomprehensible or repellent
to the parents. Correspondingly it may be reflected in
the adoption of habits and patterns of behaviour that
seem calculated to provoke confrontation. At the same
time there is often a great deal of uncertainty and fear
in the young person about the pressures of a teenage
environment. There is a lasting need for the security
which only parents who remain tolerant and reliable
in their love and support can provide. It can be a hard
time for parents. It is essential that they should not be
too protective or controlling, that they should allow and
encourage the young person to experiment in venturing
out and breaking free; yet if they give in too much and
fail to be confidently and honestly themselves in their
reactions they will fail to provide the needed security.

Fifty or sixty years ago the word 'teenager' had not
been invented and the environment in which young
people grew up was far more strictly controlled than
today. The effect was, in part, to prolong the latency
period well into the teen years, particularly in the case
of middle class children sent to boarding-schools. At
least in Britain, the sexes were normally segregated at
school. As a result children would leave school with a
degree of awkwardness and inhibition with regard to the
opposite sex which is much more rare today, and this
was combined with a degree of ignorance and naivety
about sexual matters which would astonish a modern
teenager. Yet there were advantages in this regime. A
young person was given time in which to work and
learn, to play and compete, to exercise as well as to
respect authority, in short to grow an identity, within a
protected environment. The resulting identity was indeed
incomplete and there was strong pressure for conformity

to a received set of social values, based at a remove from the Christian religion. When the boy or girl left school a lot of emotional growing up might still remain to be done. But in some respects a strong foundation had been laid, even though in other respects, particularly in cases where there was a deep splitting between mind and emotions, serious flaws were built into the structure.

By contrast, in our society today, the received ethos is one of a diffused secular humanism, with self-fulfilment as the basic criterion of value. This is a highly individualist creed and leads to a society in which great weight is given to the realization of individual potentiality. This tends to be expressed in two contrasting ways: a respect for a somewhat ruthless egoism, particularly in economic matters; and a yearning for radical but anarchic rebellion against 'the system'. The rebellion is seldom linked to any clear idea of what an alternative system might be, but it is often reflected in utopian dreams of a paradisal state, to be achieved when all constrictions on the individual have been removed; and sometimes it is reflected in outright hatred of the authorities, whoever they are. The two strains can be combined in admiration of the moody, macho, lawless hero, of the loner or the anti-hero. It could be said that the society of fifty or sixty years ago reflected the patterns of the toddler stage, with emphasis on learning self-control and acquiring a conventional super-ego; whereas the society of today tends to reflect the patterns of the preceding stage, with emphasis on the anarchic, self-regarding, narcissistic individual, with shifting boundaries of identity and fantasy. It would certainly be unwise to take these sweeping generalizations too literally, but they are sufficient to provide a useful perspective in which to consider the problems of trying to grow through adolescence today.

In sexual matters the problems of today's grandparents in their adolescence were compounded by repression, prudery, secretiveness. Those of today's teenagers are compounded by enormous pressures to perform and achieve sexually before you have had time to experiment enough in fantasy, and so before you know who you are. But fundamentally the problems do not change. The teenager has to learn to cope with strong urges, physical and psychological, which are not fully understood or under control, to cope with the very different expectations of parents and peer group, and, in the process, to discover and express a new independent identity. The process involves trying-on borrowed plumage to see whether it fits, identifying oneself experimentally with a variety of models in succession and perhaps keeping something from each. It involves competing with others, and exploring the possibilities of others. It involves falling in love, first perhaps more in imagination than in reality, but sooner or later encountering the real thing.

In a proportion of cases, especially perhaps where there is some fear of the opposite sex, the first feelings of genital desire, and sometimes the first genital explorations, may be with another person of the same sex; but even where this happens it is normally a transient phase. It is to my mind a matter of importance to the teenager's future happiness that he or she should be enabled, if possible, to grow through such a homosexual phase if it occurs; and this means that homosexual relations with or among adolescents should not be encouraged or regarded as normal and allowed to become fixated. There is a real need for young people to explore their own sexuality and that of others. A return to the repression and ignorance of the thirties has nothing to be said for it. But it is also important to preserve the years of adolescence as protected years, in which the growing teenager is enabled to explore, rebel, and discover his or her identity, including his or her sexual identity, without having prematurely to face the responsibilities of adulthood. This in turn means some limitation and control during the school years. When a young girl of school age has a baby before she or the father are ready to face the responsibilities involved, this can only be a disaster for all three of them, perhaps most of all for the baby.

It is hardly surprising that the form which troubles take in the teenage years often reflect difficulties originating in much earlier years of childhood or babyhood.

Sandra was an only child, whose father was in the Army, and she spent much of her early childhood with her grandparents. She loved her grandfather, who died when she was still very young, but she hated her grandmother. Sardra's mother was devoted to the father, and the child came very much second in her affections. She did not want another child. When the father settled permanently in England he took over the dominant role in parenting. He had affection for Sandra but was very rigid and self-opinionated. As a young girl Sandra was fairly wild, and she matured early. She quarrelled constantly with her grandmother. She took to amphetamines, barbiturates and cannabis. Together the family had some family therapy. One day, when she was sixteen, she took LSD, but this produced such a terrifying experience that she gave up drugs altogether. Soon after that she was severely beaten up and sexually assaulted by a boy she had refused to go out with. Following this she had excruciating abdominal pains, but the doctors could not find anything wrong. Her parents became unsympathetic and she ran away and lived for some months with a relative in a distant town. She only agreed to come home on condition she was 'treated as an adult'. Within a few months she married a young man who knew about her past but was not part of it. This proved a good marriage, partly, in Sandra's view, because of what she had learnt in the family therapy. They had three children. Twelve years later, however, when her husband had been away for several months (the price of holding his job) Sandra had a serious episode of depression, with a suicide attempt, and it became clear in counselling that she had deep self-destructive tendencies, perhaps deriving from the rages and lack of basic trust engendered by an unhappy infancy. She was also under continuing pressure from her father. The crises of Sandra's tempestuous teenage years clearly had earlier roots, but in themselves they reflected the normal adolescent problems of breaking free and finding an identity. They were exacerbated by her father's rigid and dominating ways, abetted by her mother's lack of sympathy. But the family did care and they did turn to family therapy when she was fifteen (at a time when this was little known). Most important of all, she had found a husband who was understanding and steady in his love, and she herself had the sense and strength to preserve a good marriage. Gradually she was able to work through to a deeper understanding of herself and so to achieve a greater freedom to take charge of her life. Always, it would seem, to be loved is the precondition of effectively venturing out and finding yourself.

This was a case in which the teenage rebellion took an explosive form. Difficulties can arise equally, however, when the opposite happens and the teenager fails to break free altogether.

Charles was close to his mother, but felt his father was always a distant, critical, self-absorbed yet controlling presence. His mother felt she had been 'held back' in her youth and she too was inhibited by her husband's attitude. This meant that, although she gave Charles love and a safe haven, she could not do much to help him to venture out; while his father (whatever his real intentions) merely distanced and intimidated him. When his younger brother was born, and later a younger sister, Charles seems to have reacted by clinging more closely to his special relationship with his mother and keeping his brother and sister out of it. Thus the child's need at the Oedipal stage to establish boundaries and an independent identity was incompletely met. He was probably inhibited in part through fear of the effect of conflict on his vulnerable mother. As a teenager Charles was rooted more at home than at school. After good 'O' level results he unexpectedly failed his 'A' levels completely and would not take them again. He said that at nineteen it would have been much too early for him to leave home and go to university a long way away.

At twenty-six he was still living at home, his social life provided almost entirely by the church in which he had grown up and which was, in some respects, for him an extension of home rather than part of the outer world. He worked as a librarian. His brother, less close to the mother, had found a job which suited him and had been able to break away without difficulty. Meanwhile his mother had been developing greater strength and independence and this was causing some strain in the home with her rigidly unchanging husband. She was encouraging Charles to move out of the house and to develop his rather tentative relationships with girls. Charles was still curiously passive and neutral. He felt he did not know who he was. He was not interested in choosing his own clothes, or in his own car (though he did surprise himself by eventually learning to drive). He was used to having many decisions taken for him and became 'stressed up' when he had to take them himself. He recognized that he had a lot of growing up still to do, in order to find himself; and he did not find the prospect easy.

For the younger schoolchild in the period of latency, ideas of religion or politics tend to be adopted uncritically from

parents or teachers or from the conventions of the peer
group, and such ideas seldom play a large part in the
child's life. In adolescence, however, they may play a
much more important part, as children strive to find
and place themselves as individuals. In breaking free
of their parents they may rebel against the religion,
or sometimes the lack of religion, in which they have
been brought up. They may take their religion more
seriously, they may undergo conversion experiences, or
they may become dedicated to social or political causes
with youthful idealism and energy. Where some rebel
against the ideas of parents, schools and authorities,
others may find security in adopting and developing them
with a full personal commitment. But in some degree
they are still trying out roles, ideas and enthusiasms,
and their dedication can shift and fluctuate with some
rapidity. All are exposed much more directly than before
to the pull of the fashionable values of the world around
them, as reflected in the media. The need to be in the
swim, and to be liked and admired by others of your own
age group is still strong. Conventions still have a major
influence on the teenager's ideas, though they may not
be the same conventions as before.

One point of some interest is the fact that when
teenagers reject and drift away from the religious or
other ideas of childhood, their understanding of the ideas
they are rejecting can easily become fossilized. As a result
of this, years later, the adult's conception of what he or
she is talking about in these fields can still be childishly over-simplified. This in turn can create barriers
to understanding in later life. Also, more importantly,
it can lead in various situations to feelings of fear, guilt
or aggression which are inappropriate and destructive,
because they are rooted in a powerful but more or less
unconscious mythology which has not been integrated
into the adult thought world.

CHAPTER TWO

I WANT TO BE ME: THE ADULT WORLD

Venturing Out (6): The Young Adult

The end of adolescence, as we usually conceive it, comes when young people move physically away from home and either begin to earn their own living, or embark upon higher education. A college or university still provides, in some respects, a protected environment; and of course young adults sometimes go on living in the parental home, whether of necessity or because that is what they like. Every case is different; but perhaps the essential mark of the change is that young adults are expected by society to look after themselves, take full responsibility for the consequences of their actions, and so to act as reliable and consistent people within the social reality that surrounds them. They are venturing out into a world which they did not make or choose, they have to survive in it, and that means that they have to compete and they have to conform. Even if you are determined to make your career as a rebel, you will need to find other rebels and co-operate with them; moreover all that you think and do will necessarily be shaped by the realities of the society you are rebelling against.

There are two immediate consequences. First, young adults will build on their strengths and, so far as possible, conceal or tuck away their weaknesses. This is not generally a conscious or deliberate process, but it is a natural reaction to circumstances. Secondly, the

kind of personality, or at least outer personality, they
develop will be shaped to a great extent by other people's
expectations, whether those of their immediate boss, or
those created by the climate of the organization in which
they are working, or those of the peer group of other
young adults among whom their social life is carried on.
Some of the freedom and scope for individuality which
they enjoyed as teenagers and students has to be given
up. They find themselves in a more authoritarian and
competitive environment, a throwback in some ways to
earlier times, with many consequences for adult adjustment or otherwise.

Success at work will give power to your elbow in the
jostling of the peer group and the shifts of its pecking
order; and competition now has an added dimension
because this is, above all, the time for seeking a mate.
Every young adult has a need to establish some kind of
niche in society, to achieve a degree of self-esteem and
confidence, and (in most cases) to find the right mate,
one with whom he or she can build a secure home, a firm
base from which more venturing out will be possible. But
some will wish to establish themselves, in their own eyes
and those of others, as sexual stars or sexual predators,
rather than as home-makers; and the images that society
admires, as reflected in the media, may encourage or
discourage various forms of behaviour. The accent of
modern Western society on individual self-fulfilment has
a powerful effect on the expectations that young adults
build into their ideas of themselves and the models they
follow today.

As Erikson has put it, much of adolescent sex life is
'of the identity-searching kind'. 'It is only now', he says,
'that *true genitality* can develop': and this is precisely
because with adulthood comes real responsibility. The
young adult 'is ready for intimacy, that is, the capacity to
commit himself to concrete affiliations and partnerships
and to develop the ethical strength to abide by such
commitments'.[1] These include not only mutual sexual

commitments, but also close relationships and loyalties of many other kinds. Correspondingly, if the young adult does not have a sufficiently clear and strong sense of identity, he or she may feel threatened by such commitments, and this can lead to 'a deep sense of isolation and consequent self-absorption'. In this fashion, we may suggest, elements of narcissism rooted in a much earlier stage of life can be reactivated, and these may well underlie patterns of both sexual isolation and sexual promiscuity.

If you are successful as a young adult, you can become strongly established within a few years, with a good job and the respect which comes from that, some economic security, a spouse, perhaps young children, and a home and possessions. As you grow on, the peer group of friends from which you emerged becomes gradually less important, and with it some (not necessarily all) of the interests in sport or entertainment, religion or politics which the peer group shared. You may develop a new set of friends, connected with your work, your neighbourhood, your own special interests, or, if you have children, other young families. You are probably still essentially concerned with establishing yourself, still building on your strengths and accommodating yourself to the expectations of others; but as confidence grows you may become more self-assertive. You have less to do with your parents. As you drift away from idealistic politics or religion, your views may seem to be more related to maintaining the *status quo* from which you have benefited. Partly for this reason, you may be reluctant to question yourself, your aims and your motives, too deeply.

Many young adults will not be so successful, but they too will find themselves ensconced in some niche in society, even if it is one which leaves them discontented and resentful. They too will find the friends of their youth pairing off and scattering, while they develop new focuses of interest and friendship. They too will probably still remain preoccupied with the problem of establishing themselves in the world, financially and socially, in ways which match, at least in some degree, the image they have of themselves. They may have tried and failed more than once to get the job they wanted or the partner in love for whom they yearned. If they are not too successful, they are more likely to agonize about themselves, but in doing so they are perhaps more liable to blame others for their plight, or to project their resentment on to society, than at this stage to question themselves in any deep way – for that is a process which puts the coherence and effectiveness of one's very self at risk.

Finally there will be some young adults who fail altogether to establish themselves at this stage, becoming the casualties of society, problems to themselves, their relatives, the doctors, the social services or the police. These are tragic cases. Sometimes they are the victims of their own weaknesses, which in turn may be rooted in difficulties unresolved at earlier stages in their lives. But sometimes also they may be sacrifices to the selfishness of others climbing on their backs, or to the ruthlessness and callousness of social institutions. The pecking order still operates in a multitude of situations, and still demands its victims, butts and scapegoats. These people's need is essentially to be helped, if at all possible, to equip themselves for making a new start in the adult world. Where that is not possible, their need is for their family or their society to give them some protected place where they can be useful and can find enough love to live by.

These paragraphs have done no more than sketch a broad framework of possibility, within and around which the path of each unique life is mapped out. What young adults discover and establish in venturing out into the world is an initial self, reflecting the strengths they have been able to mobilize in the face of the needs and expectations they have encountered – consequently a self cast in a mould formed primarily by the external environment. There is a strong tendency to stay with this self, developing and extending it where opportunity

offers, resisting any pressures which threaten to break
it down, repressing out of consciousness any conflicting
pressures from within. This is for the good reason that
any breakdown of the initial self is liable to put at risk
all that has been built up so far. In practice, with many
people, great cracks are opened by the changes and
chances of life, by failure, misjudgment or redundancy
in the work place, by quarrels, jealousies and rivalries,
by illness and tragedy, broken marriages and broken
relationships, by inability to maintain the facade that
is required. But generally in these years a person's
effort in the face of difficulty will be to try to patch up
the initial self in some new form without too radical a
change. Often indeed the adult self established in these
years will continue fundamentally the same throughout
the rest of a person's life. At this stage it is usually
only those who get into deep trouble, whether through
external circumstances or, more often, as we have seen,
through weaknesses deriving from unresolved difficulties
at earlier stages in their lives, who may be forced to dig
up the foundations and try to start again.

Venturing Out (7): Maturity

As we have noted, the initial self established in early
adulthood can sometimes remain much the same in
essentials throughout the rest of a person's life. This
is most likely to be the case when the young adult has
been successful in his or her career, has invested a good
deal of pride in it and sees no reason to change. Then
such development as does take place may be chiefly a
matter of greater confidence and self-assertion, reflected
in an exaggeration of what is already there, rather than
the emergence of anything new. A business tycoon or a
newspaper proprietor who has built up his empire in a
certain style is perhaps more likely than some others to
fall into this category. In a different context the same
might be true of a simple countrywoman in a relatively

stable and unchanging rural society, where a traditional
pattern of life does not give much opportunity for change,
and those who have fitted well into it will continue to do
so, at least until age and incapacity take their toll.

These are the 'once-born', as William James called
them, 'developing straight and natural, with no element
of morbid compunction or crisis'.[2] At their best these are
people of simple goodness and harmony of life, built on
basic trust and an unselfconscious sureness of themselves and acceptance of others. In the Christian tradition the type of such a character is the Virgin Mary.
But saints of this or any other kind are always rare,
and the possibility of 'developing straight and natural'
is much harder to find in a society changing so fast that
patterns adapted to the world in which you grew up as
a child may have little relevance to the world of your
maturity. The 'once-born' person in such circumstances
is more often one who clings stubbornly and fearfully
to the defended self which first enabled him or her to
survive and perhaps to flourish, but who can only do so
at the price of running away from self-knowledge. This
means using mechanisms such as those of denial and
projection (which we will consider in more detail later
on) to escape from hard reality – that is, from truth, the
healer – and to continue in a comforting fantasy. This is
one way of maintaining a coherent self, but the cost to
yourself and others is liable to be high.

In practice, more often there comes a time when the
self which we have built up in our early years as an adult
seems to fail, and life seems to lose its meaning. This is
a sort of mid-life crisis which can occur in many different
forms and at widely different ages, from the late twenties
to the onset of retirement. It can be a single, decisive
crisis resulting in a radical and permanent restructuring
of the self, but it is not always so. It can take the form of
a recurrent malaise and a recurrent search for a renewed
identity. It can affect those who have been successful,
but whose success has turned dry in the mouth. Perhaps

more often it follows upon some failure in a career, some
blighting of ambition, some humiliation in love, some
breakdown in a marriage or other relationship, some
disillusionment of political ideology or religious faith.
Sometimes it happens when the world grows away from
us, as perhaps with a dedicated wife and mother once
her children have moved away, or with a man forced to
take early retirement. Whatever the circumstances, its
essential characteristic is that we begin to question that
initial image of ourselves which was built up largely in
response to the demands of necessity and the expectations of others, or, perhaps, in reaction against them.
We find ourselves no longer comfortable with that image.
It doesn't seem to fit, yet we have no other. Our mind
turns to the longer-term, to matters of life and death.
We begin to wonder about the values and objectives we
have so far taken for granted; and we may begin to look
for something else.

This process usually begins in a fumbling, unconscious
way, and may never go much further. But often it does
break the surface and become a conscious search for
a renewed identity. This is the process of becoming
twice-born, which I see as the way in which we make
progress towards finding our true selves. Fundamentally,
though it may not be recognized as such, it is a religious
quest, one which is never completed this side of the grave.
Jung once wrote in a famous sentence: 'Among all my
patients in the second half of life – that is to say over
thirty-five – there has not been one whose problem in
the last resort was not that of finding a religious outlook
on life.' And, importantly, he added: 'This of course has
nothing to do with a particular creed or membership of
a church.'3 We are dealing with something fundamental
in human nature, the quest for wholeness, healing, sal-
vation – three words which at a deep level coincide in one
meaning.

It is at this stage of life that Jung's account of human
personality can be particularly illuminating. His theory

of 'individuation' is to my mind a largely successful
attempt to describe the phenomenon of discovering the
true self in its psychological aspect. The underlying
image with which he works is, like Freud's, that of
a sort of container within which the psychic energy
or libido wells up. There are three levels within this
container, that of the conscious ego, that of the personal
unconscious, and that of the collective unconscious. In the
collective unconscious instinctual psychic energy is channelled through highly generalized structural patterns of
the mind which Jung calls archetypes. These deeply
embedded patterns or tendencies are, he believes, the
product of biological evolution and common, at least in
potentiality, to all the human race. Although they emerge
into consciousness only rarely, and then indirectly in
symbolic form, they are constantly active through the
collective unconscious in shaping and energizing the
ways in which each of us copes with life.

According to this model the psychic energy is in part
channelled into the conscious activities of the ego; but this
inevitably involves the one-sided development of some
elements of a person's potentiality, adapted to the environment in which he finds himself, and the repression
of other opposed elements. There is a law of opposites
whereby the more one side of a person is developed in
his conscious life, the more the opposing side of his nature
gains strength in his unconscious. This undeveloped and
unconscious side of his nature Jung calls the Shadow.
(In some of his later writings Jung partially identifies
the Shadow with evil tendencies in the person; but this
leads him, as I believe, into muddle and contradiction.
I remain with the earlier, more strictly psychological
version, according to which it simply represents the
unconscious counterpart of the conscious ego. It was in
relation to this version that the theory of individuation
was developed in Jung's book *Psychological Types*.[4])

Individuation is defined by Jung as the process of
forming and specializing the individual nature. In his

terminology the self embraces both the conscious and
the unconscious, repressed sides of the psyche. To realize the true individual it is necessary to bring out
repressed elements and integrate them with the conscious elements; and this in turn can only be achieved
through an upheaval, often of shattering impact, which
involves the sacrifice of the 'differentiated function' and
the establishment of the 'transcendent function'. In our
terms this means giving up the initial pattern of the self
with which we first found our place in the world, and
adopting a new pattern, one which according to Jung
will emerge from the collective unconscious through the
mediation of some symbol which is deeply significant for
the individual. The form which this upheaval takes will
inevitably depend on the person's past history, on what
has been tucked away into the unconscious, on all the
hang-ups and all the unfinished business of the past, as
well as on the problems and crises of the present. But if
the process is successfully carried through, it leads, Jung
says, to a sense of reconciliation and acceptance: 'It is as
if the leadership of the affairs of life had gone over to an
invisible centre . . . and there is a release from compulsion
and impossible responsibilities.'[5]

The reconciling pattern is an expression of what Jung
calls the archetype of the self, which he also identifies
as the image of God as expressed in that particular self.
He recognizes, however, that the process is not without
its dangers; for giving up the initial pattern of the self
means taking down defences and brings with it a risk
of disintegration. It can also lead to the flooding in of
other archetypal forces, representing other sides of the
self, which have their place as parts of a whole, but which
can bring disaster if they take one-sided possession of
the person.

It is curious and interesting that Jung seems never to
have fully recognized (or perhaps never wanted to recognize) how closely his theory of individuation parallels
the idea of being reborn or renewed as it appears in the

New Testament. In St. John's Gospel, Nicodemus is told
by Jesus:

> 'In very truth I tell you, no one can see the kingdom
> of God unless he has been born again . . . You ought
> not to be astonished when I say "You must all be
> born again." The wind blows where it wills; you hear
> the sound of it, but you do not know where it comes
> from or where it is going. So it is with everyone who
> is born from the Spirit.'[6]

It is as if we have to give up the old self with all its pre-
occupations, and be reborn into a kind of weightlessness,
before we can be set free to be swept by the wind of the
Spirit. Developing a closely similar line of thought, St.
Paul says that if we are to be born anew our old self has
to die first:

> Have you forgotten that when we were baptized into
> union with Christ Jesus we were baptized into his
> death? . . . We know that our old humanity has been
> crucified with Christ, for the destruction of the sinful
> self, so that we may no longer be slaves to sin . . . Sin
> shall no longer be your master, for you are no longer
> under law, but under grace.[7]

The characteristic sign of the new life is freedom, 'the
glorious liberty of the children of God'; for sin is the
domination of the part over the whole, while grace
reflects the free gift of the Holy Spirit, who is the
Spirit of the whole – the wholeness of each individual
within the wider unity of the whole creation.

This is the process of being transformed by the renewing of your mind, of which the purpose, in St. Paul's
words, is:

> to equip God's people for work in his service, for
> the building up of the body of Christ, until we all

attain to the unity inherent in our faith and in our
knowledge of the Son of God – to mature manhood,
measured by nothing less than the full stature of
Christ[8]

It is only through this process that we achieve our own
true self, which is the self conformed to Christ. For to put
on Christ is not to put on a stereotype. Jesus is not to be
found only in the carpenter of Nazareth. As he himself
once said, 'Inasmuch as you did it to one of the least
of my brethren you did it to me.' In St Paul's phrase,
Jesus was one who 'emptied himself, taking the form of
a servant'. He is the great exemplar of free, self-giving
love, 'the man for others'.

Am I then claiming that you have to be a born-again
Christian to attain to any sort of mature development of
the self? No. What I am claiming is that the Christian
understanding of human nature includes the statement
of a general truth about us all, one also expressed
in different terms by Jung. This is the truth that, in
almost all circumstances, to achieve a degree of maturity
requires us to break the mould into which we grew as
we established ourselves in life, and then to reintegrate
the remaining fragments, including much that was previously repressed, into a new and more coherent pattern.
And I am also claiming that there is a Spirit of the whole,
working within each one of us, who, if we heed him, will
help us through the perils of this stage to find the true
pattern of our freedom.

There are some further points to add. First, although
the process can take the form of a sudden and dramatic
transformation, as it did with Paul, it can also take the
form of a series of more limited steps spread out in
time. Every case is different. Even when there is a
sudden transformation, it may take years to work out
all the changes that flow from it. Secondly, the process
is never complete in this life – though it is easy to get
stuck at one stage or another. This maturity, which

is a sort of balance in freedom, is not a permanent possession. As soon as we feel that it is, we are in trouble. For through the changes and chances of life we are constantly moving into new situations in which we have to rediscover our freedom and our selves. The ritual of venturing out and discovering ourselves anew never comes to an end. Thirdly, this process of transformation can only be undertaken in freedom; it cannot be forced upon anyone. It needs a certain degree of 'ego strength' and it has to come at the right time. To lead someone into deep disintegration who is not strong enough to grow through it, can be disastrous. And there may be indeed some few of the 'once-born', as William James suggested, who can grow on in simplicity, 'straight and natural', to the fullness of their own freedom in Christ without any 'morbid compunction or crisis'. Not only is every person unique, but in God's love and mercy his will is expressed individually for each person.

It may seem that what I have been saying about growing into maturity has been on an exalted plane, with little relevance to ordinary lives. But this would be a mistake. A Christian is sometimes tempted to complain about a religion which calls him or her to achievement which is frankly impossible. 'What is the point of expecting me to be a saint? Can't I be just moderately good?' But the fact is that the Christian call is not to reform your behaviour, but to be a new person, a person who is truly free (and therefore conformed to Christ). None of us succeeds. Our lives are full of crumbling attempts to start again. But in fact there is no coherent alternative except embattling ourselves in the old patterns, which we know is the way of frustration. We grow a little, we find a little freedom; we crumble, we grow again. As Winnicott might say, many small failures are necessary for the development of parent and child. There is perhaps no measurable achievement, but so long as we face in the right direction and try to heed our calling, we can remain within the magnetic field of grace. In T.S. Eliot's words:

> With the drawing of this Love and the voice of
>   this Calling
> We shall not cease from exploration
> And the end of all our exploring
> Will be to arrive where we started
> And know the place for the first time.[9]

The love is vital. For it is always love which gives us our identity, which gives us the confidence to give up our past idols, to venture out and discover ourselves. At this stage we can no longer rely on the love of our parents; we have to rely on the love of our greater parent, who is God, whether directly known or mediated through the love of others. Fundamentally I do not think the situation is any different for non-Christians. When the life which we constructed for ourselves as young adults begins to run into the sand, our need is not for some patchwork adjustment of ends or means, it is for a good deal of painful sacrifice, and then for a new creation, however imperfectly it is realized, in which, under the drawing of love, we can discover our authentic selves.

It may be appropriate to end this section with a case history which illustrates a series of stages of growth towards maturity.

Jane was born at a time of stress for her mother. Her father was away starting a new job in another part of the country. The mother was alone with Jane's three-year-old brother and with no relatives to help her. The labour was prolonged and exhausting, and an impatient midwife gave the mother a sense of guilt. The baby's first few months were difficult. The mother was unable to feed her at the breast and was much preoccupied by her three-year-old's jealous demands for attention. They rejoined the father, but had to live at first in awkward circumstances in temporary accommodation. After about four months the family moved into a permanent

home, a nursemaid was found who loved the baby
and matters much improved. For some time however
both parents were stressed and preoccupied. Jane
grew up in a loving home. She was an attractive,
able girl, but always diffident and inclined to feel
herself of little value in relation to others. Brought
up a churchgoer, she underwent a charismatic 'bap-
tism in the Spirit' at university. She qualified as
an accountant and began to practise successfully.
But being an accountant 'was not me'; she felt she
had adopted this career in response to her parents'
expectations. She retrained as a nurse, and within
a few years was doing well in her new profession.
But she still had not fully found herself or found
confidence in herself. One day, while praying in a
group, she received a picture of herself in a long
dark tunnel, struggling to get out, but exhausted,
miserable and guilty, ready to give up. A few weeks
later she was anointed at a healing service and
immediately had a vivid vision of Jesus: she was
in the same dark tunnel, but Jesus as a baby came
up behind her, put his arm round her, and swept her
away through the tunnel and out into the light and
the welcome of the angels. This was a turning point.
She always called it her healing. The most crucial
aspect of it was the firm assurance of God's love
and God's caring. There was in it a clear reference
to her own birth experience, so she talked to her
mother and for the first time heard in detail about
the traumatic time of her own birth. She and her
mother were also able to talk through many other
aspects of their relationship, and this was in itself
an important and emotional experience. Although
the healing was a dramatic step in her discovery
and realization of her true self, it is significant that
it was only the beginning of a long period of spiritual
development and growing into freedom. Nor was it
in any way a final experience; the healing was not

suddenly complete. It is characteristic of those who embark with real commitment on the pilgrimage of maturity that it never reaches an end point. There is always more growing to be done.

Venturing Out (8): Old Age

Erikson includes old age as the eighth and last stage of development in his 'epigenetic chart', a stage marked by the critical opposition between ego integrity and despair, and exhibiting the strengths of renunciation and wisdom. Certainly old age has its characteristic problems and satisfactions: physical disabilities, loneliness, bereavement, yet freedom from the pressures of the rat race, ample time for leisure, and so on. But in the perspective of this study I doubt if it is appropriate to consider it a separate stage. It does not seem to me (and I am beginning to grow old myself) that it is particularly notable for interest in religion, at least in any new form. I do not think the old are particularly keen on renunciation, though it may be forced upon them; nor would it be easy to sustain a claim that the aged are full of wisdom. They sometimes have long memories and they are sometimes extremely opinionated; but that is not the same thing. I am inclined to recall Eliot's words:

Do not let me hear
Of the wisdom of old men, but rather of their folly,
Their fear of fear and frenzy, their fear of possession,
Of belonging to another, or to others, or to God.
The only wisdom we can hope to acquire
Is the wisdom of humility: humility is endless.[10]

What does strike me is that in old age the inhibitions previously imposed by fear or shame are liable to be gradually eroded, with the result that the true character of the person begins to show through more clearly. True generosity, love and sweetness of nature can become more confidently apparent in a most moving way; so, alas, can selfishness, envy, malice and all uncharitableness. It is true that it is easy, when you are old, to get stuck in a rut. It becomes more difficult to venture out and discover yourself anew in ever-changing circumstances. But although the opportunities may be reduced, the task does not seem to me to be changed in any fundamental way. It is still possible to grow through the continuing encounter with the world; and there are indeed many old people who do grow remarkably in wisdom, serenity and the capacity to live for others. It is often in old age that a strong prayer life will bear its most precious fruits. To quote Eliot again

> Old men ought to be explorers
> Here and there does not matter
> We must be still and still moving
> Into another intensity
> For a further union, a deeper communion
> Through the dark cold and the empty desolation.[11]

Bereavement and loss can strike at any age. As a generalization it may be true to say that the younger the victim is, the greater the trauma that results. But it is in old age that we experience bereavement most frequently. I do not propose to say much about it here, mainly because a number of good books have been written about it in recent years to which I have little to add.[12] Some important ideas about bereavement are now becoming widely accepted: for example the need to go through an extended period of grieving, and not to try to bury it or snap out of it prematurely; the different stages through which the bereaved person may pass; the unbelief and even delusions, the stress and anxiety, the anger, the blaming of others, the guilt and the other emotional states which often accompany our grieving; the need to avoid getting stuck in grief, living endlessly in the past; and the corresponding importance of growing through the grief to discover a new life and a new identity. Here the only point I wish to make concerns the nature of bereavement itself. In truth we are bereaved not merely of a person, but, more importantly, of the life we were looking forward to leading with that person. It is our own future that we have lost. We have to give up a whole series of stories projecting into the future which made up a major part of our anticipating self. So it is our *self* that is damaged; and it is natural for us to feel pain, frustration and disappointment. In facing this challenge, like the other challenges of life, we have to venture out into contact with a new reality, and through this contact to discover a renewed self. When so much has been pulled away, the task is daunting, especially if we are old and find it hard to begin new things. But this is where our freedom lies: 'Old men [and women] ought to be explorers.'

CHAPTER THREE

STORIES TO TELL

Self and Stories

Every time you take a decision, whether you are committing yourself for life, as in proposing marriage, or whether you are picking up a pencil from the floor, you tell yourself a story; and then, as you watch the outcome, what actually happens, you tell yourself another story. The first story is a plan worked out in your imagination, the second is a record, a registration of fact in your memory. All stories are in effect extended pictures, images of events which are spread out in time as well as in space. And the story is a unit, that is to say it has a finite shape or form, with a beginning and an end. If that were not so, you could not grasp it, you could not take hold of it as an idea in your mind.

In the case of something as simple as picking up a pencil, the whole process may happen within a split second and largely below the level of consciousness; but even so there has to be some kind of picture in your mind of the movement to be made and the purpose to be achieved; and this picture must have an extension in time as well as space. This might not be the case with the decisions which your mind-body makes automatically and unconsciously, for example, when a sudden movement makes you blink. But I am concerned here with conscious decisions in which you are exercising your free will; and I am concerned with them because in every such decision you take part as a person.

The mark of being a person is that you have a will of

your own; and that will is expressed by a temporary or responding self which emerges differently in each situation. This is the conscious self that creates or envisages the story, or the set of alternative stories from which a choice has to be made. It is a sort of temporary mobilization of relevant elements from the underlying, unreachable totality which is the whole of you.

What are these elements? The form in which they emerge is that of ideas – and ideas, I will venture to suggest, are ultimately stories, though they are stories in an encapsulated, synchronic form. Even abstract ideas are in this sense encapsulated stories. When you spread them out in sentences to grasp them, you are recognizing relationships between other ideas ordered in a conceptual space and over a step of time.[1]

Most of the ideas which make up the total psyche would seem to be memories, either memories of actual experience or memories in the form of knowledge acquired from other people or from books, television or other media. The total size of the memory store of any grown up person is inexpressibly large; but of course only an infinitesimal fraction can be recalled to consciousness at any one time; most of it is in any case beyond deliberate recall, though external circumstances can often trigger unexpected recollections of what had seemingly been forgotten. It is important to note that the mind can recall stories at different levels of generalization, either with the fine grain that remembers, for example, a particular occasion when you won a prize at school, or with the coarse grain that thinks of your schooldays as a whole.

A significant proportion of the ideas which make up the total psyche however, though they may indeed be memories, are more than memories, because they have some binding power over the decisions that you take later on. Every time you take a decision you adopt a plan which stretches on into the imagined future. If all these decisions were taken independently, great confusion and contradiction would follow; you could well decide to be in

two places at once. So the mind builds them together into
a more or less coherent structure within the total psyche,
which I call the anticipating self. The essential function of
the anticipating self is to ensure that whenever a decision
comes to be made, the temporary, responding self which
is mobilized for the occasion includes an awareness of
past decisons which may affect it and have to be taken
into account. In other words its function is to give you as
a person some *coherence* over time and so to make sure
that you do *not* decide to be in two places at once.

Broadly this means that short-term decisions have
to be accommodated to long-term ones, and particular
decisions on points of detail have to be accommodated
to more general decisions of principle. If I want to get
my hair cut, I have to fit that decision in with the fact
that I have already committed myself to catch a train at
nine o'clock and spend the day in London. I may want
to get out of making that trip to London, which means
ringing up and giving the excuse that I am not well; but
there is something in me that feels uneasy about telling
a lie. In fact one story that I tell myself does not fit in with
another story about truthfulness; and the conflict leaves
me uncomfortable.

Many of the decisions I take – the plans or stories
that I adopt – are acted out to completion, successfully
or otherwise, and thereafter they cease to be part of the
anticipating self, they just become ordinary memories.
But I have been taking decisions since babyhood, since
long before I can remember. At any time, my anticipating
self consists of a very large number of stories, some of the
most general and lifelong kind, some much more particular and short-term, all of which are fitted loosely together
in a ramshackle fashion, like a collection of overlapping
scales. They include not only the stories I tell myself, but
also stories which I tell other people in presenting myself
to them. These may not coincide exactly with my own
inner thoughts, but they nevertheless have some binding
force; I need to live up to what I claim to be. Beyond this

they also include stories corresponding to the social roles to which I am committed, whether in carrying out my job or in other contexts. These are not always roles which I particularly like, but if I fail to perform them, there will be a penalty to pay.

All this builds up a highly complex structure, more or less coherent, but only more or less, because we can never foresee the contingencies of life, and we can never foresee all the conflicts of interest, desire and duty into which we may fall. By no means all of this structure is open to conscious recall. In particular the stories which build up the super-ego, and which have a most important continuing influence upon a person's decisions, are for the most part, as we have seen, repressed out of consciousness. The same applies to memories which go back still further, into babyhood, but are no less important for that. These are not just passive memories of things that happened to the baby, but, far more importantly, choices made by the baby long ago as means of coping with different forms of stress. One example could be a pattern of retreat into despair and a sense of worthlessness and nothingness, when a baby has to cope with what seems like being deserted. Such a story can be reactivated, though without conscious recall, in the face of apparent rejection in adult life, and the consequences can be very serious. Again, in identifying with parents or others in childhood, we may adopt ideal roles, which can be guiding stories of great importance through the rest of our lives, without our being fully conscious of the fact.

How does all this work? In particular how can something be reactivated without being consciously recalled? To deal with these questions adequately it will be necessary to go a good deal further into issues of theory than would normally be feasible in the counselling room; but I believe this will make it easier to deal with other matters later. In exploring these issues of theory I will try to relate what I have been saying, to the ideas of Freud, with which many readers may be familiar. Readers who prefer to do without the theory may wish to skip the next two sections of this chapter.

Conscious and Unconscious

So far I have spoken of the *total psyche* and, as a structure within it, the anticipating self. The former is for the most part a *memory store*. I tend to imagine it as a vast terrain, the mind-manifold, built up through the consecutive experiences of our lives, over which the flakes of new experience are continually drifting down, settling on the places where they most aptly fit, but not obliterating what was there before. The manifold is ordered in two ways; first by the location of things and events on a sort of map of space and time[2] – on which I am able to place, for example, the house next door, the Persian Gulf or the Norman Conquest with equal ease – and secondly by means of classifications based on similarity or past association. These classifications are identified by marker images, which are signs or symbols such as words. It is through this system of ordering that we are enabled to retrieve items from the memory store when they are relevant to what is going on Here-Now in consciousness.

Within the total psyche the *anticipating self* is a structure of ideas linked by the fact that as plans or stories, these ideas project and fray out into the future, constraining in various ways the future decisions of the individual. The memory store and the anticipating self are however built of ideas in the form of timeless encapsulations. It is in a third structure, which I call the *arena of consciousness*, that our actual experience takes place Here-Now, in a perceptual or conceptual space as a happening in real time. This arena corresponds to what Freud calls the *perceptual-conscious system*. Similarly the anticipating self corresponds to what he calls the *ego* (incorporating the *super-ego*); and the rest of the memory store corresponds to the *preconscious* (the part from which elements can be retrieved into consciousness), together with the *unconscious* (the part from which they cannot). But the correspondences are not exact for reasons which I will explain.

Freud did not only divide the psyche into the perceptual-conscious system, the preconscious and the unconscious. Superimposed upon these three is the division into super-ego, ego and id. The *super-ego* is a split-off part of the ego and both of them include both preconscious and unconscious elements. The *id* is totally unconscious. Freud maintained that in the id there is no passage of time and no logical contradiction; it is 'a cauldron of seething excitement' where instinctual energy presses to discharge itself in a variety of directions in accordance with the 'pleasure principle'. But the *ego* is in touch with reality through the perceptual-conscious system and strives to control and organize the passions of the id rationally, in accordance with the 'reality principle'. In this task it is obstructed by the super-ego 'which holds up certain norms of behaviour, without regard to any difficulties coming from the id and the external world.'[3]

Freud's model of the psyche, developed a hundred years ago, is of the so-called hydraulic type. Instinctual energy pours into the id and works through it in divergent streams, powering in the process both the ego and the super-ego. The attempt to characterize and analyse the sources of instinctual energy or libido is one of the most controversial aspects of Freudian theory, as also of its Jungian counterpart. What I am offering instead is a model based on the theory of self-regulating systems, that is, systems with an input of matter/energy and information, and an output of regular purposive behaviour.[4] A diagram is given at fig.1 Every model or hypothesis inevitably has its limitations, but I think this one has some significant advantages.

The arena of consciousness is the arena of Me-Here-Now, in which a perceptual input, consisting of ideas

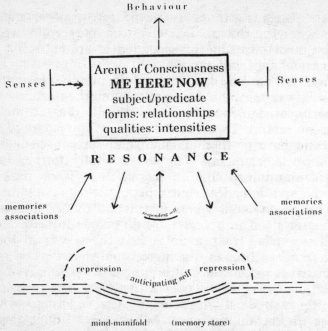

selected and synthesized from the information pouring in
through all the senses, is related to an input of ideas from
the memory store. These are ideas linked in a complex
way by similarity or past association to what is already
present in the arena and they are evoked by means of
a sort of resonance through the memory. They include
what I have called the temporary, *responding self*, which
is synthesized from relevant ideas in the anticipating
self. The combined input is organized into a succession
of scenes or predications – Now after Now after Now –
at the focus of consciousness, as seen from the position
of Me, the temporary self. So we have the experience of
Me-Here-Now in successive steps throughout a person's
waking life. Each step is in effect a miniature story, helping to build up a longer story within the comprehensive
story that each person constructs through living his or
her life.

What precisely do I mean by a *predication*? Here

we are using the language of grammar. According to
my theory the basic rules of grammar are the rules
of the structuring of consciousness; they apply to all
perception and thought, as well as to language. The
subject is the initial form on which attention begins to
focus. The *predicate* is the background (in vision, sound
or whatever) against which the subject emerges; or the
object in relation to which it moves, or remains still; or
the complement which is absorbed as an elaboration of
the subject. In this last case the predicate is the subject
itself with a difference – which may be only a difference of
time. The structure of the sentences of language reflects,
as I believe, the underlying structure of the predications
of thought, adapted to a linear succession of words – and
not *vice versa*. (The reader should be warned, however,
that this is an area of controversy in psychology and
philosophy: the model should be relied upon so far as it
is helpful, it should not be taken as final truth.)

In every predication – and this applies to perceptions
and thoughts (even in dreams) as well as to speech and
writing – a subject is related to a predicate over a step in
time. Both subject and predicate can be complex: as many
as seven or eight forms can be separately recognized and
related in one predication, one span of Now – but not
more.[5] The forms, however, are always infused with a
certain quality and intensity of sensory or emotional
colouring. We cannot think without some accompanying
flux of mood or emotion, any more than we can see
form without colour or hear a tune dissociated from any
quality or intensity of sound. It is only the separately
recognized forms at the focus of consciousness which
are rationally related together (though the predication,
once realized, can itself be remembered and stored as a
single form, an encapsulated whole). Where, then, do the
accompanying sensations and feelings come from?

I would answer this question with the aid of what I call
the musical analogy. Every musical tone has a simple
wave form, but any tuned note normally has a complex

form created by the superposition of many overtones of
different but mathematically related wavelengths upon
the fundamental tone. Normally you hear only the pitch
of the fundamental tone, the others are buried individually out of consciousness. Yet it is they, in their merged
or collective impact, which together determine the quality and intensity of the note you hear. It is a particular
proportional mix of overtones that we identify as the
sound of, say, a trumpet, a flute or a bassoon. Similarly,
as I see it, our *emotions* represent the collective impact
of innumerable ideas associated directly and indirectly
with the ideas at the focus of attention, and recalled by
means of a type of resonance from the memory store.
These ideas are not separately realized in consciousness
– there would be far too many of them – but they have
their effect simultaneously. The collective impact of the
constantly shifting cloud of associations represents the
continuing activity of the mind in its unconscious aspect.
In fact this *is* the unconscious, expressing itself in the
emotional colour of what is recognized in consciousness.
The unconscious is not a separate compartment into
which we delve from time to time; its activity is the
unceasing accompaniment of all our conscious life. The
process of resonance and recall is the basis, not only of
memory, but of imagination, exploration and fantasy,
which are essential to creative understanding, to the
identification of goals and purposes, and so ultimately
to all of our planning and action.

The fact that the individual ideas forming part of the
cloud of associations make their impact simultaneously
explains why, as Freud noted, logical relationships and
the passage of time find no expression in the unconscious.
On the other hand, as it seems to me, the unconscious
does reflect relationships of similarity of form and of past
association, since it is through these that the mechanism
of recall through resonance functions; and this is perhaps
why its natural language often seems to be one of symbols. It also follows from my account of the matter that

ideas which are at one moment consciously recognized at
the focus of consciousness can at another moment – often
immediately afterwards – contribute unconsciously to the
emotional tone of experience. (Freud indeed allowed for
some thoughts being 'temporarily unconscious', though
not in the way or on the scale suggested here.)

There remains the question of ideas repressed out of
consciousness. Certainly there are barriers, as Freud
discovered, to the recall of certain memories and fantasies into direct consciousness as units at the focus of
attention. Fundamentally, in the terms of the model I
am using, this is because they are incompatible with
some elements of the anticipating self, most commonly
elements of the super-ego which originate in early childhood. The result is that on an occasion when otherwise
they might have been recalled explicitly, they clash with
the temporary self, Me-Here-Now, and are consequently
held out of consciousness and restricted to an emotional
impact. We will consider this process in more detail
later. But the point to be made here is that the whole
of the memory store is always available to contribute
to the clouds of association which colour our experience, *including* those elements which are excluded from
explicit consciousness. This corresponds to Freud's point
that 'the barrier of repression does not extend into the id;
so that the repressed material merges into the rest of the
id' (where, presumably, it rejoins the seething cauldron
of instinctual impulses).

Emotion and Decision

Freud argued that the instinctual energy of the mind
takes two forms, that of the erotic instincts and that of
the death instincts. These are differentiated into 'object
cathexes', which are impulses towards or away from
certain kinds of objects, for example people on whom
emotions of fear, anger or love are focussed. The ego
in relation to the id is like a rider trying to control a

wild, unbroken horse, and impeded all the time by the parental interference of the super-ego. The analogy of music which I have used, however, offers a very different theory of the emotions, one which can do justice both to their infinitely subtle gradations and variability (for the particular mix of values in the emotional resonance of any moment of consciousness is unique) and also to their broad classifiability. Moments of rage or fear or jealousy have a broad similarity in their quality, just as the sounds we associate with violins or with chords of the dominant seventh, or the hues we associate with the colour green also have a broad similarity, even though every occasion of experience is unique and unrepeatable.

As an explanation this account has added plausibility because it makes use of a mechanism akin to one which we already know to be characteristic of the brain and mind. So far as the intensity of emotion is concerned, it suggests that the intensity varies according to the extent of the resonance which has been stimulated, and this too has its analogy with what we know of perception; for the intensity with which we feel a particular sensation appears to be directly related to the number of neurones in the brain which are stimulated into firing by the experience. There is of course still an unexplained transition between the patterns of neurone firings and the actual sensations or emotions of consciousness; but this brings us up against the great problem of the relationship between mind and body, which is perhaps ultimately insoluble and which in any case I have no intention of tackling here. Before moving on, however, it may be appropriate to pause and contemplate for a moment the great mystery of the human brain, which the neuroscientist Gerald Edelman has described (with perhaps a reminiscence of some words of Albert Einstein) as the 'most complicated arrangement in the known universe.'

The musical analogy can point towards a new understanding of the way in which conscious and unconscious experience are interwoven: how the same element which at one moment is at the focus of attention can at the next moment be lost to consciousness, while it still contributes to the emotional quality and intensity of the experience. Beyond this it can suggest something of the way in which unconscious activity can affect the direction of the conscious mind. In free association, as Freud recognized, the mind follows the pleasure principle. Ideas in the memory store have a certain threshold of stimulation, some are more easily stimulated than others, and the mind follows the line of least resistance until it is brought up against the reality principle. Every qualitative tinge of experience, in imagination as well as in reality, can be sensed as pleasant or unpleasant; and as soon as the focus is on a story leading into the future this becomes itself a focus of desire or aversion. It is through such a mechanism that the mind identifies its goals. As different possibilities are considered, each attracts a different weight of desire or aversion. As different plans are considered for achieving particular goals, each reflects a different weighting for feasibility which dilutes its attraction to a greater or lesser extent. Decisions are eventually taken through the ordering and balancing of emotions. In this way a great desire can be opposed by fear of the consequences of pursuing it, or by misgivings of conscience. Even if it prevails, its attraction may be weakened if the attempt to achieve it looks unlikely to be successful.

The fact that it is primarily the emotional balance which determines the decisions that we take has one particularly significant implication. It means that the temporary self, present on every occasion of consciousness and representing the anticipating self or ego, does not always get its way when decisions have to be taken. For a person's emotional life is governed by the resonance of the whole psyche, including aspects which are repressed out of explicit consciousness. What we decide to do is not simply determined by the need to accommodate any new plan to the existing patterns of the anticipating self as they emerge in consciousness on that occasion. Our decisions are by no means always rational.

Nevertheless the need to maintain as far as possible the integrity of the anticipating self plays an extremely important part in the conduct of a person's life. As we have just seen, the anticipating self does not finally determine my actions, for ultimately it is the whole of me that decides what I do. Within the process of decision, however, it is the anticipating self which defines the self I am trying to be and also the aims I am consciously trying to achieve. If I do something which conflicts with these aims – for example if I run away when I like to think of myself as being brave – I begin to weaken or disintegrate the anticipating self, and this is always felt as painful and frightening. The final aim which is built into me as a living creature is to survive, but if I am to achieve this I have to adopt a series of plans and roles which are adapted to the environment in which I find myself, take account of my own past history and capabilities, and are reasonably coherent with each other. The function of the anticipating self is to make this possible. It is the only continuing coherent structure within the psyche representing the self, and if it becomes disintegrated, disaster threatens. Consequently the mind has a strong tendency to erect defences against such a risk.

There is a sense in which every new plan adopted by the anticipating self, adding a new story to the greater story of my life, also adds a new bit of outer crust to my defences; for once a decision has been taken and a new plan adopted, there is always resistance to altering it again. The stories we tell ourselves and the stories we tell others about ourselves become part of an anticipating self which, as we can now see, is also a self-defence system. If the plan deals with a particular small matter only, or if it is a short-term plan without long-term implications (like whether we are to go for a walk this afternoon), there is no great difficulty about changing it. But if it goes deeper, the issue can be much more complicated.

Recall that the structure of the anticipating self is a hierarchy, with the particular and short-term stories accommodated to the generalized and long-term stories. If one of the deepest-lying layers in the hierarchy has to be shifted, this can have a disintegrating effect on all sorts of other stories that have been fitted into it; and the emotional reverberation of any attempt to shift it is correspondingly intense and painful. Add to this the problem that many of the deepest-lying stories are repressed out of the field of direct consciousness, and we can begin to see the roots of those difficulties over growing up into a free and mature human being which were the subject of our first chapter.

Why should any of our stories be repressed? I think there are two answers to this question. First, repression is itself a defence mechanism. Given the vicissitudes of childhood, and the unpredictability of our lives, it is almost inevitable that some of the general ideas and attitudes we adopted at one time or another no longer fit into the broad contours of our anticipating self as it has since developed. Achieving a degree of coherence and consistency in our responses is what the anticipating self is about, and so it is convenient and necessary that we should be able to tuck away into unconsciousness some of the stories that would otherwise lead to open conflict and incoherence. But secondly, there is the special case of the repression early in life of the admonishing parent figures of the super-ego. It seems to me that this repression is not a defence so much as a necessary precondition, if the child is ever to become independent.

A baby can only act according to its own needs – a necessary state of selfishness. It learns only gradually to separate itself from those who minister to its needs. But life involves living with others and that has to mean the frustration of some of our desires in the general interest, which is also, in the end, our own interest. One of the roles of parent figures is to be the agents of this frustration. The fact that the admonishing and

punishing aspects of the parent figures are internalized
in the form of the super-ego brings a representative, as
it were, however primitive, of the general social interest
into the mind of the child; and this it is which enables the
child to begin to grow into an independent social being.
But if the child were constantly conscious of internal
parent figures saying one thing, while its own parents
in daily life were saying something else, it could only
be left in confusion. So the larger than life super-ego
parent figures are repressed into the unconscious, and
with them a variety of memories and fantasies of which
we are convinced they would disapprove, especially those
with a sexual or aggressive flavour. There is always a
complicated mixture of accurate perceptions and imagined disapprovals. And, sadly, many children do have
severely adverse experiences in their early lives.

Because they have been repressed out of consciousness
in this way the parent figures of the super-ego remain as
the small child imagined them, simplistic and often, as
Freud noted, harsh and cruel (presumably because it is
the frustrating parent, not the approving and encouraging parent, who needs to be internalized). The fact that
they are repressed enables the child – and later the adult
– to face the world as a single personality, not a confusing
medley of differing persons. But from the unconscious
they can still influence the conscious understanding
indirectly and emotionally – often through feelings of
guilt. When they conflict with what the conscious mind
is planning or doing, the effect can be deeply disturbing.
For conflict within the anticipating self is precisely what
threatens disintegration. If you look at the mind-body as
a self-regulating system, the function of painful emotions
is precisely to signal such a conflict without actually
breaking up the self, and so to drive the individual into
doing something about the situation.

Geoffrey was the son of a dominant mother (who
also dominated his father). He had an elder brother,

taller and cleverer than himself, who was always putting him down, though Geoffrey still looked up to him admiringly. Geoffrey had an underlying confidence rooted in the feeling that he was his mother's favourite, but he also learned early that the best way to avoid being pressured by his mother or bullied by his brother was to keep his head down and keep his deeper thoughts and feelings to himself. He developed a pattern of coping which was based on acting an outwardly complaisant part while inwardly keeping his own counsel. He grew up with a certain sense of inferiority, but a strong inward ambition to succeed. He became an actor for a time, then turned to business and became a marketing manager, though he still at times had a sense of only acting the part. He married a shy girl, younger than himself. At first the marriage went reasonably well, but there was never much communication between them. They had two sons, but in middle life, when the children had grown up and moved away, Geoffrey began to find himself in trouble. He lost his job, partly because he had not been able to establish any close personal understanding with his colleagues, and he was not able to find anything comparable to replace it. Meanwhile his wife had grown in confidence and dominance and she became increasingly exasperated because he communicated and responded so little. His confidence had been further shaken by the loss of his job and he tended to put up the shutters and to retreat further into the way of coping which he had originally developed in dealing with his mother. The growing crisis led him to come for help. He readily came to understand and acknowledge the roots of his trouble. He saw that he needed to open up with his wife and talk about his own feelings and problems in a way he had never done before. Only in this way could he hope to get a response from her and lay the foundation for

a deeper relationship. But this would make him
vulnerable and the idea filled him with fear. He
really liked being what he called his 'secretive
self', listening to others but saying as little as
possible himself. To grow further into freedom and
maturity he would have to shift a deep layer of his
anticipating self, taking down his defences before he
could be renewed. He recognized this and he firmly
wanted to move and grow; but the process was very
difficult and painful for him. He had first to grow
the inner strength and motivation to face the need
for change.

Lies and Deceit

Our analysis suggests that the mechanisms of repression
serve an essential need in helping to preserve the coherence of the anticipating self or ego, but they do so at no
mean cost. The anticipating self is built up piecemeal
over a considerable time, helping us to cope with the
world in which we find ourselves. In general, if the world
of our upbringing has been a tolerable one and does not
change too fast or too radically, our coping mechanisms
– which are in effect our broad stories about ourselves,
building up the main contours of the anticipating self –
will generally enable us to get by. As time passes and we
encounter new situations, especially in adolescence and
young adulthood, we add new stories and slip them over
the old; but often the old patterns are still there and still
colour our emotional reactions without our realizing it.
As the stress builds up, radical change in the anticipating
self may be needed to cope with it. But the resistance is
strong. We try to preserve our old self and we have a
series of weapons with which to do so. One is repression.
Another is denial, when we simply believe what we want
to believe rather than what is in front of us. A third is
projection, when we delude ourselves into discovering
in other people those objectionable aspects of ourselves

that we can't accept. A fourth is withdrawal, when we simply avoid facing the issue. What all these defence mechanisms have in common is the attempt to escape from uncomfortable truth, whether about ourselves or about others or about the world. They all involve a degree of retreat from truth into an illusory world of our own. They are lying stories.

This leads to the conclusion that if we are to become free and mature adult people, what we need is to face the truth. That is indeed what I believe. Truth is the healer. But truth can also be a destroyer. The need to maintain the integrity of the anticipating self is still paramount if we are to survive as sane people with coherent wills of our own. You do not help people by trying to tear down their defences before they have found the understanding to know who they are and the strength to be themselves. Where, then, do we find this understanding and this strength? The answer, as the explorations of the first chapter of this book suggest, is through knowing that we are loved and valued. Only then do we have enough basic trust to make ourselves vulnerable, and open ourselves to change.

But there is more to it than that. There is a subtle and remarkable discussion of the nature of truth in the eighth and ninth chapters of St. John's Gospel, in the course of which Jesus says to a group of the Jews: 'If you continue in my word, you are truly my disciples, and you will know the truth, and the truth will make you free'. The Jews find this annoying and patronizing, for they are descendants of Abraham and consider themselves to be free already. Jesus answers them: 'I know that you are descendants of Abraham; yet you seek to kill me, because my word finds no place in you.' As the altercation continues, he says some ferocious things:

'Why do you not understand what I say? It is because you cannot bear to hear my word. You are of your father the devil, and your will is to do

your father's desires. He was a murderer from the
beginning, and has nothing to do with the truth,
because there is no truth in him. When he lies, he
speaks according to his own nature, for he is a liar
and the father of lies . . . He who is of God hears the
words of God; the reason why you do not hear them
is that you are not of God.'[6]

Both in this chapter and in the next what is striking
is that Jesus is continually misunderstood, and he is
misunderstood because his hearers are deceiving themselves, believing their own stories, not his 'word', which
is the word of God. They 'cannot bear' to hear his
word, because they want to follow the devil's desires
as their own.

It is difficult not to feel some sympathy with the Jews
as they are faced with the tremendous, yet cryptic claims
which Jesus makes. We ourselves are often in their
position. But what Jesus is saying is that they do not
need sympathy, the truth is there in front of them, in
the word he brings from God, in his very self. In the
prologue of the Gospel, Jesus himself is described as
the Word, and elsewhere in the Gospel he says: 'I am
the way, the truth and the life'.[7] What is this truth? In a
real sense the whole Gospel is about bringing the reader
again and again to a point where he can himself make
the vital leap of understanding. The truth is the Word.
It cannot be wrapped up in propositions, in many words.
Yet one thing is clear. The word is spoken. We *can* all
hear it; but when we do we must obey, as Jesus himself
obeyed; and paradoxically it is only in obedience that we
can be set free. The trouble is that we have to give up our
other obediences before we can follow Christ who is the
light of the world.

In the terms of this study, we have to give up the
false stories with which we deceive ourselves. We can
have the courage to do this because we will not be left
in disintegration, we will be held in God's love. I have

already referred earlier to the story told in the third
chapter of the Gospel about the mysterious encounter
of Jesus with Nicodemus, who came to see him by night.
Nicodemus is told that if he is to see the kingdom of God,
he must be born again 'of water and the Spirit'.

> 'That which is born of the flesh is flesh, and that
> which is born of the Spirit is spirit. Do not marvel
> that I said to you "You must be born anew." The
> wind blows where it wills and you hear the sound of
> it, but you do not know whence it comes or whither
> it goes; so it is with every one who is born of the
> Spirit.'[8]

This, as I see it, is an assurance that if we are born anew
we will cease to be led by pride, fear or desire, that is by
the flesh; we will be blown by the great wind of the Spirit
of God and so enabled always to put the kingdom first in
our lives.

Another way of putting it is that we will be under grace.
I will be following up that thought later on, but at this
point we have to note that St. John goes on immediately
to speak of God's love. 'For God so loved the world that
he gave his only Son that whoever believes in him should
not perish but have eternal life.'[9] We can trust God's love
made known through his Son. Then he continues:

> 'This is the judgment, that the light has come into
> the world, and men loved darkness rather than light,
> because their deeds were evil. For every one who
> does evil hates the light, and does not come to the
> light, lest his deeds should be exposed. But he who
> does what is true [in the Authorized Version 'he that
> doeth truth'] comes to the light.'[10]

We are back again with the self-deceiving stories that
people tell themselves. And John reminds us of a point

which has not so far been noticed. Time and again we
do things that are not what we really want to do,
things which are dictated by the emotional tides of the
unconscious, rather than by the anticipating self. If we
acknowledge the fact, we find ourselves in a painful state
of remorse. But time and again we do not acknowledge
the fact. We find an excuse for ourselves, we tell ourselves
another story to avoid having to face the truth. This is
added uneasily to the anticipating self and so we descend
the spiral of self-deception. 'Men loved darkness because
their deeds were evil.'

It is self-deception, not conscious deliberate falsity,
that continually leads us into darkness. In chapter 9
of the Gospel, Jesus says to the man born blind, in
the hearing of the Pharisees 'For judgment I came into
this world, that those who do not see may see, and those
who see may become blind.' When the Pharisees ask if
he was talking about them, he replies characteristically:
'If you were blind you would have no guilt; but now that
you say "We see", your guilt remains'.[11] It is significant
that those who have been convicted by the law seldom
accept their guilt. We are told by prison psychiatrists that
habitual child-molesters who have done untold damage,
sometimes to scores and even hundreds of children, will
generally persuade themselves that they were loving the
children and doing them a favour. It is not just the things
we do wrong that are the matter with us; much more
important in practice, as this Gospel brings out so well,
are the stories we use to avoid facing the truth about
ourselves, so that we do not need to change. And often
as the story of Jesus makes sadly clear, we do not
merely find innocuous excuses, we project what we do
not want to face upon others and so justify ourselves in
persecuting them 'even unto death', in order to preserve
our own righteousness. In terms of religious practice it
does not get us very far merely to identify and confess the
little acts of selfishness or malice or bad temper that we
can easily reject as not characteristic of our real selves.

It is more important, and much more difficult, to strip off some of our layers of self-deception, the stories we tell ourselves to justify staying the way we are, and so to risk discovering and acknowledging something of our own deeper motivations.

CHAPTER FOUR

I WANT TO BE FREE

Evil

Looking at the gospel has brought us up against words like sin and evil, concepts which may seem to be at odds with the tendency of modern psychotherapy and counselling to try always to avoid moral judgments. But in practice people are often deeply worried about guilt and remorse, blaming and being blamed. To deny sin is in effect to deny human freedom and responsibility. Yet to blame or condemn another human being for his or her sins is to arrogate to oneself a superiority which it is dangerous for anyone to dare to claim. How are we to approach these questions?

It is logical to begin with evil. The traditional Christian teaching about it is expressed by St Augustine:

> These things we call evil, then, are defects in good things and quite incapable of existing in their own right outside good things ... A defect is something contrary to nature, something which damages the nature of a thing – and it can do so only by diminishing that thing's goodness. Evil therefore is nothing but the privation of good. And thus it can have no existence anywhere except in some good thing.[1]

Evil is not positive, it is negative, it is what damages good: and, what is good is the whole positive creation. In the words of Genesis, 'God saw everything that he had made. And behold it was very good.'

If the world, as created, was very good, why then is there evil in it? The problem of reconciling the fact of evil with the fact of creation by a loving and almighty God has stretched the minds of prophets, theologians and philosophers since the days of Job, and I cannot hope to resolve it here. But neither can I leave it aside; for anyone who encounters the injustice and cruelty of human destiny must ask: 'Why?'; and constantly the cry of 'Why me?' makes itself heard in the counselling room. What can the counsellor say?

The first thing he can say, I suggest, is that we have to face the truth and accept that the world *is* unjust and cruel. It is most obviously so in the case of such impersonal disasters as fire, flood, earthquake, famine, disease and accident. But injustice and cruelty can grow out of the structures and pressures of human society, which are largely inherited and beyond any individual person's wisdom or capacity to perfect. There is also injustice in the genetic inheritance of many unfortunate people, just as there is cruelty in the grim circumstances in which many have to grow up and live. We must refuse therefore to put the blame for all the evil in the world on man. Jung traces back to the second century the doctrine that all good comes from God and all evil from man. But God is responsible for the world he created, and his shoulders are broad. It is no way out to put all the blame on Adam or, worse, on Eve. Nor, for that matter, on Lucifer and the fallen angels. Rather we can follow St. Paul, who says in the Epistle to the Romans:

[The created universe] was made subject to frustration, not of its own choice but by the will of him who subjected it, yet with the hope that the universe itself is to be freed from the shackles of mortality and is to enter upon the glorious liberty of the children of God. Up to the present, as we know, the whole created universe in all its parts groans, as if in the pangs of childbirth. What is more, we also,

to whom the Spirit is given as the firstfruits of the
harvest to come, are groaning inwardly while we
look forward eagerly to our adoption, our liberation
from mortality.[2]

Death is the destroyer, and mortality here stands for all
the futile destruction of the good which happens in the
world. But in the end death itself will be destroyed and
the created universe will be redeemed. As Paul wrote
elsewhere 'The last enemy that shall be destroyed is
death.'[3]

Paul gives us no explanation why the universe was
made subject to frustration. Similarly Job was given no
explanation for the injustices inflicted upon him. But at
the end of the book, after 42 chapters Job addresses these
words to God:

... I have spoken of things which I have not understood, things too wonderful for me to know.
    Listen, and let me speak. You said: I shall put
questions to you, and you must answer.
    I knew of you then only by report, but now I see
you with my own eyes.
Therefore I yield, repenting in dust and ashes.[4]

In either case the conclusion is that we cannot understand God, yet we can trust him. This is very near the
core of religious faith. God is beyond our grasp, but God
is, and God is good.

This is an area in which neither science nor philosophy
can take us very far. It has to be a matter of faith, even
if your faith is that the world is meaningless, black and
absurd. Different forms of religion or moral philosophy
have offered different explanatory myths to account for
good and evil. It would be far outside my present purpose
to discuss them in detail here, but I will allow myself a
few dogmatic comments. The first is that a God of love,
mercy and justice cannot at the same time be a God

who consigns his children to eternal torment because of failures for which he himself as creator carries much of the responsibility. The second is that any theory based on reincarnation or the wheel of rebirth into this world runs into insuperable difficulty when it comes to defining what precisely it is that is reincarnated, what the relationship is between the individual in one incarnation and the same individual in the next. The third is that there is much force in the argument that the possibility of human sinfulness, and so of human responsibility for evil, is the other side of the coin of human free will. The story in Genesis of Adam and Eve eating from the tree of the knowledge of good and evil can perhaps best be understood today as a story of the dawning of man's reflective self-consciousness, his first recognition of his freedom, and so of his responsibility for the consequences of his actions. This argument has recently been extended by an interesting suggestion made by some physicists that the evolution of the universe itself in accordance with the laws of nature, depends on the existence of a degree of freedom or randomness, without which 'time's arrow' itself could not come into being.[5]

The fourth comment will be rather more extended, since it concerns an extremely influential psychologist, and one whom I much respect, C.G. Jung. In some of his later writings, notably *Aion*, Jung argued against the traditional view that evil was to be regarded as the privation of good, the *privatio boni*. In his view it was a positive force, though he never defined it, except as the opposite of good. He developed this dualism into a complicated theological myth, of which one aspect was the replacement of the Holy Trinity by a Quaternity, in which Satan made a fourth member, opposite Jesus Christ. This is linked in to the Jungian theory of the reconciliation of the opposites as the aim and outcome of the process of 'individuation' to which I referred in Chapter One. It is my belief that Jung's argument, so far as evil is concerned, is invalid because it is based on a mistake, his failure to distinguish an opposite from a negative. The opposite of North is South. The negative of North is everything that is not North. (Technically this is described by logicians as the distinction between a contrary and a contradictory.)

'Psychology', Jung said at one point, 'does not know what good and evil are in themselves; it knows them only as judgments about relationships. "Good" is what seems suitable, acceptable or valuable from a certain point of view; evil is its opposite.'[6] This is a relativistic view of good. But Jung is not consistent. He clings to the dogma that in some extra-psychological sense there is an ultimate dualism of good and evil and he links this to the opposition between the conscious and the unconscious, the ego and the shadow (which muddles up unfortunately his perfectly good psychological theory of the shadow). Other differentiations of opposites follow, 'for it turns out that all the archetypes spontaneously develop favourable and unfavourable, light and dark, good and bad effects. In the end we have to acknowledge that the self is a *complexio oppositorum* [a weaving together of opposites] precisely because there can be no reality without polarity.'[7]

Jung develops a view of man as inherently combining good and bad elements. The process of individuation or growing into maturity involves a fuller integration of these elements through the differentiation and subsequent weaving together of the opposites. This view of man is matched by a view of God as also including evil elements and going through a similar process of differentiation and weaving together of opposites. The various divine figures in Jung's pantheon are none of them omnipotent. His God is a sort of Grand Vizier out of the *Arabian Nights*. And so inevitably he has to envisage in addition a sort of shadowy God behind all gods, whom he calls *Moura* or *Dike*, Fate or Justice. It will be clear that I think his theology is a mess.[8] In psychology I think that his theory of the *complexio oppositorum*, though important, is also deeply flawed. Individuation does involve the integration of discordant elements, but not through a miraculous reconciliation of opposites, rather through a reconstruction of the anticipating self. This reconstruction can include not only the adoption of new ideas of the self, but also the specific abandonment of old ideas, which are *not* integrated, but relegated to the memory store. (It is not true, incidentally, that there can be no reality without polarity. A case could be made for the proposition that in human terms there can be no consciousness of something positive without at least the possibility of a negative; in other words we cannot recognize a figure or outline except against a background. But that does not mean that figure and ground are polar opposites.)

Jung's venture into theological speculation grows out of some shrewd and cogent criticism of the popular Christianity of his day, but it singularly misunderstands, or fails to engage with, the central realities of the faith, such as the incarnation, Christian rebirth, justification by faith, and God as love. Jung has a good psychological theory of falling in love, but there is a great gap in his psychology where love in the wider sense is concerned.[9] I have devoted attention to him here because his influence, direct and indirect, has been so great in recent years; but not all of it, in my view, has been for the good.

Is there any conclusion, then, to draw about evil? I have suggested that evil is negative, anything that works for the destruction of the good. The existence of evil is part of the condition of the world. It is not all man's fault, though man is responsible for what he chooses in his own free will to do. The possibility of evil seems to be a consequence of the degree of freedom that there is in the world. We can speculate that God has created the kind of world we see in order to allow humans to grow in their own freedom into the full harmony of love and goodness, and so to share in the divine life, in the resurrection of Christ. But we cannot see into the mystery. We can only

trust. And why should we trust? For a Christian there
can be only one answer. God *loves* his world, however
appearances may sometimes suggest the contrary. He
has shown us this by sending his Son to share our life
and our pain, and to demonstrate in his living and dying
that the true divine nature is that of self-giving love. And
he has vindicated his Son by raising him from the dead.

As I have said, it has to be a matter of faith. Dr.
Margaret Spufford, writing out of half a lifetime's experience of physical and emotional suffering, concludes that,
in the face of evil, academic theology can be of little help.
In the worst times the one thought which seemed to her
to carry weight was that God cares enough to suffer
with us.[10]

Sin

Jung was originally drawn into his theological specula-
tions because his clinical experience brought him to the
opinion that the church set moral standards which were
impossibly high and so led to failure, guilt, hypocrisy and
all manner of psychological ills. It must be conceded at
once that on the face of it he had a strong case. 'Be
ye therefore perfect', said Jesus, 'even as your Father
which is in heaven is perfect'[11]; and it is true that
over the centuries some versions of Christianity have
misinterpreted such sayings in a way which makes every
human hopelessly guilty of mortal sin and so deserving of
hell fire. This has indeed done great harm. Jung however
drew, as I believe, the wrong conclusion, by proposing in
a curious, muddled way that it was right to have a bit
of evil integrated into your personality, and that God
too was a sort of integration of good and evil. But his
critique can only be answered through a much deeper
understanding of sin and grace than popular Christianity
has usually been able to demonstrate. I believe all the
materials for this are available in the New Testament
and certainly many good teachers have used them. For

my part I am not qualified to write as a theologian, but if, as a psychologist, I am to deal with the problems of sin, guilt, blame and forgiveness, I have to venture into this territory.

The ideal of health and the criterion of moral value which is accepted implicitly, not only by most of the schools of secular psychotherapy and counselling, but also by most of Western society, is the humanist ideal of self-fulfilment – alternatively described as self-realization, self-actualization, self-improvement, personal growth, and so on. What is desirable in life is to realize your potentialities, doing things which stretch and develop your capacities and give you pleasure. For most people most of the time this is an implicit assumption to which little thought is given. Much of the time it makes fairly obvious sense and is hardly open to objection; indeed it is closely allied to the concept of growth into maturity used in Chapters One and Two of this book. But it conceals considerable difficulties.

The root of the trouble lies in the fact that human beings do not live on their own. They depend on others, especially in childhood, and they cannot realize their potentialities in isolation. How then do you balance the wants and needs of one individual against those of another, or against those of society as a whole. Humanist moral philosophers have worked out complex schemes for determining in a logical and consistent way the allocation of rights and duties which will lead to a just society and the greatest good for the greatest number (a good example is John Rawls's remarkable book *A Theory of Justice*[12]). But moral philosophers do not agree with each other and their systems do not much affect the consciousness of ordinary people.

In the broadest terms there are three ways of approaching the problem. The first is that of people who think they know what the ideal society is and how to get there. For them, once the social and economic revolution has been achieved, individuals will cease to be alienated and will

grow into the ideal socially-responsible pattern. Such
was the approach of Karl Marx. Significantly Marxism
assumes that human beings are naturally good and will
develop in good directions once the oppressive structures
of class and state are removed; indeed ultimately the
state will wither away. Marxist solutions have been
tried in many countries and have generally produced the
opposite of what Marx hoped for. It is hard for anyone to
recommend them now.

The second method of approach is based on a recognition that some humans have much greater potential
than others and their self-realization is justified at the
expense of others. The great man in his defiance achieves
authenticity of the only kind that matters. Nietzsche is
perhaps the greatest prophet of such an approach. It is at
present deeply unfashionable in the West, but in certain
times and places, when people look for heroic leadership,
it can have a powerful psychological appeal.

The third method of approach, which is widely dis-
seminated in the West today, reflects an optimistic and
permissive view of human nature. It is seldom explicitly
worked out and formulated, but its values are implied in
much of the work of modern humanistic psychologists,
who have had an important influence in forming popular
values, especially in the United States. Interestingly Carl
Rogers, one of the best known of them, and distinguished
as perhaps the founding father of modern counselling,
has had the courage, and perhaps naivety, to spell out the
philosophical foundations of his work in a book published
in 1978. In this book, *Carl Rogers on Personal Power*,[13]
he argues that there is in every organism 'an underlying
flow of movement toward constructive fulfilment of its
inherent possibilities'. This is a 'trustworthy function of
the whole organism'. All that is needed is to set it free.
This requires genuineness and openness in all relationships, an attitude of 'unconditional, positive regard', and
empathic understanding. It implies an accepting, non-
directive approach not only in psychotherapy but also in

family relationships, including child-rearing, and marriage, in education, politics and international affairs.

There is a great deal that is of real value in the Rogerian approach. But Rogers vastly underestimates – in fact he hardly mentions – the forces of evil and destruction in ourselves and in the world. He assumes with a degree of blindness that if people are open enough, all sorts of problems can be solved by consensus. He implies that ultimately any commitment can be abandoned if something better turns up, and he explicitly advocates what amounts to a doctrine of serial and simultaneous marriage. He does not face the fact that the 'person-centred' approach, if carried to its extreme, must lead, and has led, to a world of isolated atomic individuals, with commitments to each other which are no more than matters of temporary convenience, as each does his or her own thing. Rogerian 'process persons' (his own most apt description) are in the end people deeply uncommitted to anything except themselves, endlessly adaptable, but precisely because they are lowest common denominator people. Rabbi Jonathan Sacks has put this point very clearly – although he is speaking, not specifically about Carl Rogers, but more generally about the condition of modern society:

> It is not that we have stopped thinking morally altogether. It is, rather, that our moral imagination is bounded by three central themes – autonomy, equality and rights – the values that allow each of us to be whatever we choose. The central character of our moral drama is no longer the saint or the hero, but the free self, unencumbered by attachments, unobligated by circumstance, freely negotiating its temporary contracts with others: Frank Sinatra singing 'I did it my way'.[14]

It is worth taking note of the extremes to which this kind of thinking can lead, because in practice it is

so widespread today. Many secular psychologists are
far more realistic in their view of human nature than
Rogers. Nevertheless for all of them, as for the moral
philosophers, the concepts of evil, sin and guilt are
hard to handle; and I think this is primarily because
of two assumptions which often strongly influence their
thinking. The first is that human nature is basically good.
The second, which reflects the prevalent scientific world
view, is that we are all creatures of our inheritance and
our environment and so we are not to blame for what we
do wrong.

There is however also a third factor which it is salutary
for any Christian to take into account, namely that the
word 'sin' has often become loaded over the centuries
with a weight of inculcated guilt, which a psychotherapist
will often rightly see as the product of a powerful and
persecuting super-ego – of religious as well as parental
origin – rather than the product of true self-knowledge.
In too many cases the sense of sin has been falsely
rooted in a vindictive, punishing, super-ego concept of
God. Virtue becomes attached to self-blame and the
acceptance or imposition of punishments, as a way of
placating the deity, and these then become substitutes
for any true transformation of the self – indeed they
become defences against it. When this sort of thing
happens, the result can be extremely destructive, not
only for the individual concerned, but also for others
on whom his or her guilt, anger and rebellion may be
projected.

A significant proportion of the personal problems of
patients or clients with whom psychotherapists and counsellors have to deal are related to excessive self-blame
and desperately low self-esteem. It is therefore understandable that they tend to be uncomfortable with the
idea of sin. But I believe it is most important that
the reality of sin should not be denied or buried in
euphemisms. We need rather to understand it better,
so that we can be set free from it; and here I believe the

Christian faith has much to contribute. If we have free
will and are responsible for what we do with our lives,
then we are inevitably face to face with sin; for sin is what
happens when we fail to use our freedom and so act with
true responsibility, in other words as *whole* people. Sin,
I believe, is a slavery to part of ourselves, the tyranny of
the part over the whole.

The fact remains however that it is still not a straightforward matter to formulate a coherent and defensible
Christian view. Not many people today can accept the
idea of the total depravity of man (at least in the obvious
sense of that phrase), and I am certainly not among
them. Again it seems to me impossible to deny that we
are largely shaped by inheritance and environment, and
are therefore not totally responsible for the wrong we do.
The Christian tradition however, incorporates a number
of strands which I believe have to be drawn together
here. First, human beings are made in the image and
likeness of God. They have the potentiality to be so
transformed that they can share in the resurrection
of Christ and so in the life of God himself. Secondly,
we live in a fallen world, which means not only that
there is a great deal of evil in human existence, but
also that our nature is flawed, we are all, at least
some of the time, inescapably sinners, doers of evil,
ourselves. Thirdly, God is loving and merciful, he has
redeemed us, which means that he has bought us out
of our sinfulness. Fourthly, we have free will, and to
avail ourselves of the redemption freely offered we have
to repent, which is to turn to God and be set free from
our sins. Fifthly, God cares for us and wants us to be set
free, but if we turn away from him, we incur guilt and
we inevitably bring upon ourselves evil and ultimately
destruction.

I now want to try to show how these ideas can be
coherently understood in psychological terms today, and
how the Christian view of sin, guilt and forgiveness
relates to the secular humanist approach. I mentioned

three possible versions of humanism. I shall in effect be
suggesting that Christianity can be regarded as a fourth
form of humanism, but a *paradoxical* humanism. Christ
came that men 'might have life, and that they might
have it more abundantly';[15] yet we have to die in order
to live, we have to be obedient in order to be free. How
can this be?

Grace

'Whosoever will save his life shall lose it; but whosoever
will lose his life for my sake, the same shall save it.'[16]
This is Luke's version of a saying of Jesus which occurs
in one form or another in all four Gospels, and no less
than five times in all. And the word which is translated
as 'life' is *psyche*. The psychology of the New Testament
is centred not on any detailed analysis of mind or soul
or spirit – and *psyche* can be translated by any of
these words – but rather on bringing about a process
of radical change, psychological and spiritual, in the
individual person.

This change is associated with such phrases as 'being
transformed by the renewing of your mind', 'being born
again', 'losing your life and finding it', 'the perishing of
the outward man while the inner man is renewed day
by day', 'putting on the new man', 'adorning not the
outward person but the hidden person of your heart', and
so on. What, then, is the purpose of the transformation?
The key word here is freedom. 'If the Son makes you
free', says St John, 'you will be free indeed'.[17] St Paul
cries out 'For freedom Christ has set us free'.[18] Through
Christ, says St Paul, we can inherit 'the glorious liberty
of the children of God'.[19] What are we to be free from?
From sin. And what is sin? The compulsion to do what
you don't want to do, a form of slavery. As suggested
already sin represents the tyranny of the part over the
whole, so that the whole loses its self-determination.
The sinner is a doer of evil, either to himself or to

others. He is led by the flesh (or, as the Revised English
Bible puts it, by the unspiritual nature), instead of
being led by the Holy Spirit, who is the Spirit of the
whole; and the whole is more than the individual, it
is the whole body of Christ; in the words of the Book
of Common Prayer it is 'the mystical body of thy Son,
which is the blessed company of all faithful people'.
And what is the end result of being governed by the
unspiritual nature rather than the Holy Spirit? 'Sin,
when it is full grown', says St James, 'brings forth
death.'[20]

In fact the process we are talking about, although from
one point of view it is a matter of psychology, a transformation of the psyche, reaches far beyond psychology.
It is a matter of life and death. 'While we are still in
this tent', says St Paul, 'we sigh with anxiety; not that
we would be unclothed but that we would be further
clothed, so that what is mortal may be swallowed up
by life'.[21] The purpose of our being on earth is seen as
being to live the life of the kingdom; and this is a new
kind of life which overcomes death and stretches into
eternity.

As the first three Gospels make abundantly clear, the
concept of the kingdom was at the very centre of the
teaching of Jesus Christ. He returns to it again and
again. The fourth Gospel does not often use the language
of the kingdom, but with its different imagery of light
and darkness, life and death, it brings us continually
up against the selfsame mystery. The Father reigns.
We his children are to look for his kingdom and obey
his will. 'As Moses lifted up the serpent in the wil-
derness, so must the Son of man be lifted up, that
whoever believes in him may have eternal life.'[22] In this
obedience, following Christ we find our freedom and our
true selves. When we are disobedient we are in sin and
bondage and darkness. When we repent, when we turn
back to obedience, we are forgiven and set free, we come
to the light.

The idea of a king whose service is perfect freedom has
in it an element of apparent paradox. The kingdom of
God is too deep a concept to be pinned down in rules or
fixed into propositions. Instead of giving us statements
and precepts, Jesus taught in parable after parable. We
find the kingdom likened to a man who sowed good seed,
to a treasure hidden in a field, to leaven, to a grain of
mustard seed, to a merchant in search of fine pearls, to
a net thrown into the sea, to a king who wished to settle
accounts with his servants, to a householder who planted
a vineyard, or to a king who gave a marriage feast. These
are only a few of the many comparisons he draws. He
makes it clear that to understand the meaning of these
parables requires a special sensitivity or openness: 'He
who hath ears to hear, let him hear'. And in his own life,
death and resurrection Jesus enacted the greatest, most
mysterious parable of all – one which is nevertheless in
its essence still, as always, a parable of the kingdom.

In the kingdom we have to put first our obedience to
the king; we have to be guided by grace. But what does
this mean? Jesus doesn't use the word grace himself. It
is very much a word which his followers used: the grace of
our Lord Jesus Christ, and I want to suggest that grace is
closely associated with the kingdom. It is through God's
grace that we can know God's will and do it; and, as St.
Paul said, we have that grace 'through the redemption
which is in Jesus Christ'.[23] It is his bequest to us. He not
merely taught about the kingdom, he left us the means of
grace, the means of living in the kingdom; and this grace
cannot be separated from the activity of the Holy Spirit
himself.

Grace however remains an elusive concept; and in
trying to get a little deeper I will turn to yet another,
rather precarious, parable. The kingdom of heaven is
like a man riding a bicycle. When we ride a bicycle we
have to keep moving and we have to keep our balance.
So long as we do this, we are free and we can ride where
we like. If we don't, we fall off. Similarly in the moral life

we are on a pilgrimage in which we have to keep moving
and keep our balance; in other words we have to avoid
the entanglements of sin. And sin itself is a negative; it
is whatever makes us fall off.

Riding the bicycle, we stay upright by being aware of
the force of gravity and putting first our obedience to
gravity. We must not be too timid to get moving, or we
fall off. We must not stiffen our necks or strike attitudes,
or we fall off. We must not lurch or grab after whatever
takes our fancy to left or right, or we fall off. Similarly in
the moral life we have to seek first the kingdom and God's
righteousness, as Jesus enjoined. If our first concern is
fear, particularly of what others will say or do, we fall into
sin. If our first concern is to strike the attitudes of pride
or ambition or conceit or self-deception, again we fall into
sin. If our first concern is with our wants, our greed, our
lust, our anger, with what we are going to eat or drink or
wear, we fall into sin, we fall off the bicycle. All sin could
be described as an excess or exorbitance of fear or pride or
anger or desire, or of some unholy mixture derived from
these. Whenever we put something else first, something
other than God, we lose our balance, and so we lose our
sensitivity to grace.

Fear in itself can be useful; we all need to be prudently
afraid when a real danger threatens. Similarly we all
need to have a proper pride, in the sense of an idea
of ourselves on which our integrity can be based. We
all need a capacity for the anger which mobilizes our
strength against a threat of destruction or invasion. And
we cannot live without wanting things. It is not these
motives in themselves which do the harm, it is putting
them first, letting them take us over. Because when we
let them take us over we lose our true selves, we lose
our balance, we fall off the bicycle, we are obsessed, we
are enslaved. Sin is always a slavery. And it is always
evil; it always does harm to us, and often does harm to
others too.

But how can we avoid it? How can we avoid losing

our balance and becoming enslaved? Certainly we cannot
do it by means of willpower – what Simone Weil called
'the muscular will' – or by following rules. This lies at
the core of St Paul's tortuous, but extremely important,
argument about the law, which he goes so far at one
point as to call 'the ministration of death, written and
engraven in stones'.[24] There is no rule that can save
us. You don't stay upright on the bicycle by carefully
following the rule that when you turn to the left you
must lean over to the left – however valid and correct
that rule may be. It is something much more rapid and
subtle than that. There are sensors in our bodies which
constantly monitor the direction and force of gravity, and
it is because unconsciously we are constantly aware of
gravity that we can ride freely. The moral life is much
more difficult, but the principle is the same. We have to
be continually aware of the kingdom – not just of rules
and commandments, but of something much more subtle
and liberating, which is the grace of God.

God's free gift of grace is always with us, like the force
of gravity, so that we can know when we are in balance
and when we are not; the test is that of freedom. If we
let ourselves be governed by grace, if we put first that
awareness, and so 'practise the presence of God', we are
in the kingdom and we are free, and God's love can flow
through us. Here is the transformation of life and the
renewal of mind of which St Paul writes. This is how
'for freedom Christ has set us free'. 'Through Christ
Jesus the law of the Spirit of life set me free from the
law of sin and death.'[25] We die to the old self, we put on
the new. Under grace we are no longer being conformed
to the world, we are being conformed to the mind of
Jesus Christ, who was always in perfect obedience to
his Father.

God does not normally give us guidance which tells us
directly what to do, for that would be to take away our
free will. Rather he helps us to discern when what we are
planning or doing has the taste of sin and when it has the

taste of grace. We can learn to know by a sort of negative feedback when we are under grace and when we are not. This is what the theological concept of discernment is about. And just as it is the instant, subconscious, fearless obedience to gravity which allows us to ride the bicycle freely, so it is the instant, subconscious, fearless obedience to grace which sets us free as human beings to be our true selves.

This is the gospel, the good news. To follow Christ involves sacrifice, but it is a sacrifice of the old self with its priorities of pride or greed or fear or envy or malice, in order to find a new self who is our true self, no longer enslaved, but genuinely free and genuinely loving. This sacrifice, however painful, is not ultimately a constriction of life, it is a way to abundance of life. But it is never an easy option. We are still on our pilgrimage. To be in a state of grace is to be a saint, for however fleeting a moment – and I do not believe that even the greatest saints were saintly all the time. The transformation is never permanent and fully achieved this side of the grave. The old self keeps coming back. But it is vital not to give up. There is no halfway house between sin and grace, and this is the reason why the teaching of Jesus in the Sermon on the Mount seems to us to be so extreme: you are either *perfectly* in balance and so riding free, or you have fallen off (or you are on the verge of falling off).

Riding a bicycle does not come naturally, we have to learn and practise how to ride; and similarly we have to learn and practise the awareness of God's grace; and we can work on this by means of prayer, which is precisely developing our relationship with God. We all sin, it is part of the human condition to be sinful; but God knows that. The word grace is also synonymous with mercy and forgiveness: 'O taste and see how gracious the Lord is.' If we pick ourselves up and turn back to God, the forgiveness is there already. In St Paul's words, 'For God has consigned all men to disobedience, that he may have mercy upon all.'[26] God expects us to sin, but he is working constantly to help us to learn, in freedom, not to; and it matters enormously that we should succeed, since in so far as we do, we find ourselves co-operating with him in building the kingdom, and in so far as we fail we help to pull it down.

Addiction

I have suggested that, apart from its religious significance, the teaching of the New Testament makes extremely good sense in psychological terms. In this respect it can be applicable to anybody. It would be confusing and objectionable however to force religious terminology on a non-believer; and the problem therefore arises of how you are to talk about such concepts as grace or the life of the Spirit to someone for whom religious language is meaningless or an obstacle.

If he or she is prepared to use the language of Jung, we are already halfway there. When Jung, in dealing with what he calls individuation, speaks of the leadership of the affairs of life going over to a new centre, with the result that there is a great release from compulsion, he is, I believe, not far from the concept of being born anew and thereafter being blown by the wind of the Spirit, steering by grace. He makes it clear that there is no halfway house between the old centre and the new centre, and that this dramatic change cannot be achieved without sacrifice of the old self, otherwise the 'differentiated function'. Dr. Anthony Storr emphasizes the extent to which Jung thinks of the psyche as a self-regulating system which has an inherent tendency to seek its own equilibrium. Jung himself speaks in some contexts of a *spiritus rector* in terms which correspond closely with the Christian concept of the Holy Spirit who, in St Paul's phrase, 'speaks in the inner man', and whose operation, as I have already suggested, cannot be separated from the grace of God. (Jung identifies the inner image of

God with the unifying archetype of the Self. He always
tends to find God within, and this leads him towards a
relativism under which everyone creates his own God or
gods. It seems to me that he offers what is equivalent to a
theology of the Holy Spirit but unfortunately without any
complementary theology of the Father and the Son. The
same comment could be made about much of the 'New
Age' thinking of today.)

For those who are not Christians and not Jungians I
can best explain what I mean in terms of the theory of the
anticipating self, described earlier. The broadest contours
of the anticipating self are formed by the stories we adopt
about ourselves which are of the longest span and the
widest generality; and such stories often take the form
of 'ideal roles', through which we identify ourselves with
particular ideally conceived persons, the heroes or saints
of our imagination. When a Christian puts on Christ, he
is adopting an ideal role which, as I have said earlier,
is not a stereotype, but rather the perfect example of
self-giving love, Jesus 'the man for others'. Whereas
humanist theories of value usually involve an attempt to
establish some set of priorities, some kind of hierarchy of
human ends, this one involves subordinating all human
ends to the will of God. Yet the will of God is almost a
kind of emptiness, since it is not expressed in any set of
rules, it has to be sought anew on each occasion; and then
it is identified not by positive command so much as by
negative feedback; it is marked by the sense of freedom.
We are great self-deceivers, and it is possible to deceive
ourselves over the will of God. In the Christian view we
can only 'test the spirits', as St. John said, by setting
the story we are telling ourselves against the story of
Jesus Christ, and so measuring our intentions against
the criterion of self-giving love.

The idea of balance or equilibrium is always central to
any attempt to discern right and wrong in these terms,
since without balance there is no freedom and we fall
off the bicycle. The root meaning of the word translated

as sin is 'missing the mark'; and we recognize that only
the archer who is perfectly poised can aim straight and
hit the target. But it should not be forgotten that there
can be no balance without gravity, and there can be no
moral balance without the moral equivalent of gravity,
which we have identified as grace. In the Christian view
this grace is the free gift of God, universally available
to those who turn to God. This does not mean that it is
only available to Christians, for wherever there is true
self-giving love, there is Christ. As we are told in the
Epistle to the Romans, 'when Gentiles who have not the
law do by nature what the law requires, they are a law
to themselves . . . They show that what the law requires
is written on their hearts.'[27]

In these terms sin is to be regarded as an addiction or
attachment which prevents us from being free, and so
prevents us from recognizing the truth of the situation
in which we find ourselves. The state of grace or freedom
is thus in a sense one of detachment, or non-attachment,
a fact recognized in many religious traditions, but still
easily subject to misunderstanding:

> There are three conditions which often look alike
> Yet differ completely, flourish in the same hedgerow:
> Attachment to self and to things and to persons,
>   detachment
> From self and from things and from persons; and,
>   growing between them, indifference
> Which resembles the others as death resembles life,
> Being between two lives – unflowering, between
> The live and the dead nettle.[28]

Dr. Gerald G. May of the Shalem Institute in Washington,
who has had long medical experience of people with
addiction to drugs or alcohol, is prepared to use the
term with a much wider application. He takes the
view that the range of possible addictions is almost
limitless. He found that he was himself addicted not

only to nicotine and chocolate, but to 'work, performance, responsibility, intimacy, being liked, helping others, and an almost endless list of other behaviours'.[29] In fact he extends the word to cover every sort of 'normal' desire or craving, and it seems right to him to do so because all such cases, when they become exorbitant, can, in his experience, exhibit the classical symptoms of addiction: dependency, withdrawal symptoms, tolerance (the need for increasing amounts), and also self-deception, loss of willpower and distortion of attention (getting things far out of proportion). He concludes that 'to be alive is to be addicted, and to be alive and addicted is to stand in need of grace'.

This presentation could seem like just playing with the meaning of words, but I think it is more; it puts everyday facts of life in a new and useful perspective. It helps me personally to recognize that I am addicted in all sorts of ways; and I think the recognition is salutary. What he is saying restates the theological doctrine of detachment, the freedom which comes from being at God's disposal under grace. The opposite of detachment and freedom is idolatry and bondage, otherwise sin. And in secular terms sin can be recognized as addiction.

Dr. May goes on to examine the great variety of attachments or addictions (in his wide use of the word). He emphasizes that 'no addiction is good; no attachment is beneficial'. He also develops the idea that we can have aversion addictions, otherwise repulsions such as 'phobias, prejudices, resistances or allergies'. These are marked by symptoms which are mirror images of normal addiction symptoms – intolerance rather than tolerance, approach symptoms rather than withdrawal symptoms, and so on. I think he is right in principle about aversion addictions, but I have some reservations about his treatment of the idea. In some cases at least the problem, I believe, is what I would call a counter-addiction, otherwise addiction to a form of behaviour originally adopted as a counter-measure to an addiction: I think some cases of *anorexia nervosa* fall in this category. Depression on the other hand is, I believe, fundamentally a device we adopt to deaden the pain of rejection. If we accept that we are hopeless and worthless, we may be miserable but there is not much that can give us any further hurt. In many cases, therefore, addiction to depression can perhaps be seen as a straightforward addiction to a pain-deadener – though it is of course no less a serious matter on that account: automatic self-blame becomes the means by which we avoid examining what we *can* do to help ourselves.

After considering the variety of attachments, May proceeds to discuss the psychology of habit formation and the way addiction attacks not only the will (it 'splits the will in two, one part desiring freedom and the other desiring to continue'), but also the person's self-esteem (primarily through repeated failures to get free). He then considers the working of the brain and the physical basis of addiction. Interestingly he shows that it is rooted in the body's necessary capacity for habituation, and can apply to habits of mind as well as to substance addictions.

In this sense the word 'addiction' can certainly cover neurotic fears, different forms of pride and other false images of the self, including the excessively low self-esteem which afflicts many people. It serves not only to give a useful meaning to sin in secular terms, it helps also to correct and extend the Christian understanding of sin, which is often a distorted one. Many of our most damaging addictions, as was suggested in Chapter One, are rooted in coping patterns acquired very early in our childhood. In certain situations these can be brought to life again, inappropriately and against our conscious will, tangling up our reactions in the present. It may seem odd to call such unfortunate addictions sinful, since they are not the result of conscious adult choice (and it may even be as well to avoid using the word sin in such a connexion for fear of misunderstanding). But in truth, if sin can be seen as addiction, there is no sharp boundary to be drawn between sin and sickness. We tend automatically to connect sin with blame, and Christians are sometimes too quick to blame. But we need to remember the saying of Jesus: 'Judge not, that you be not judged.' We are all liable, Christians and non-Christians alike, to be too harsh in judging and rejecting ourselves, as well as others. We need to love ourselves, sinners though we be, before we can begin to love our neighbours. And we need to acknowledge that we will never overcome our sins or addictions in the strength of our own 'muscular will'. Only grace will set us free. Conscience, in the sense of the harsh, judging parent-figures of the super-ego will never do so.

Conscience

We cannot do without the super-ego, built out of the basic parental stories of right and wrong which put a moral orientation into our lives. Working instantaneously, emotionally, unconsciously, it provides us with an automatic pilot which strongly colours our immediate judgments and gives us a first approximation to steer by. But we must not be governed by our automatic pilot. If we use the Transactional Analysis categories mentioned in the section on 'The Toddler' in Chapter One, it is the Adult's judgment which must ultimately be in charge. With many people it is quite easy to recognize when it is the Parent who is reacting, and when it is the Adult or the Child. In many circumstances the simplistic Parent reaction may be appropriate and sufficient; but when people adopt their parent stories as their own and rationalize everything else to fit them, they end by cutting themselves off from the real world.

What is necessary if we are to grow into maturity is, in traditional religious terms, to purify our conscience. It is worth remembering that the fundamental meaning of the word conscience, and one which it still retains in French, is consciousness, especially consciousness of oneself. It reflects the idea of ourselves that we want to live up to – in Freudian terms the ego-ideal. It is important therefore, if we are to lead coherent lives, that the unconscious stories, in particular the unconscious ideal roles, in our anticipating self should not be in conflict with the plans and roles that we consciously adopt. This is one reason why an intellectual conversion in the moral life is not sufficient, we need to be emotionally converted as well to whatever the new conception of the self may be; and this means that the emotional resonance from the super-ego should be in concord, not in dissonance with the new ideas. If there is conflict here, showing itself, for example, in confusion, indecision, anxiety or depression, it can sometimes be sorted out by counselling or psychotherapy. But there are older, more traditional methods, ways of prayer, meditation, confession, 'examination of conscience', discernment and spiritual guidance, which can be powerfuly effective.[30] Perhaps the crucial first step is to become consciously aware of the conflict, and so of the need for change in oneself. Once this is clearly in focus, it becomes possible gradually to change the stories and adjust the priorities of the anticipating self.

The direction of change, if the arguments of this book are valid, should be towards a full identification of the anticipating self with the story of the self as free under grace – which means for the Christian, identification with the mind of Christ, the ideal role of Jesus. Whereas our relation to the admonishing parent figures of the super-ego is primarily one of fear rather than love, the process of purifying our conscience is essentially one of bringing in the 'perfect love' which 'casteth out fear'. With love comes the obedience which is genuinely trusting and free, that of a happy child. In our relationship with our own parents there was probably something of this, but it was mixed also with fear, with a wary alertness to their possible anger and disapproval. As we discover our true selves we grow in fearlessness and in the motivation of love.

In his remarkable book *Awakenings*[31] Dr. Oliver Sacks

describes the case histories of a number of patients
imprisoned over many years by the rigidities, tics, twist-
ings, freezings and catalepsies of post-encephalitic Par-
kinsonism. These patients were miraculously brought
back to health by the drug L-Dopa – though often for a
pitiably short time. Their stories can perhaps help us to
identify the characteristics of the true self. 'The qualities
of the first awakening', he says, 'are essentially those of
innocence and joy – like an anomalous return to earliest
childhood: the Awakened, in this sense, irrespective of
their age, come to resemble the "once-born" of whom
William James speaks.' The patient 'now feels at ease,
and at one with the world ... There is a great sense of
spaciousness, of freedom of being.' 'Unease and discord
– in the most general of senses – are the sign and source
of returning disease.'

Innocence, joy, spaciousness, freedom, these are among
the signs that we are being our true selves. And probably
all of us have had some experience of this true health,
enough at least to recognize it and so to be able to use it as
a criterion for knowing whether we are free or not. At any
one time the temporary self, through which we face the
situation in front of us, draws on only a small fragment of
the total structure of the anticipating self. The resonance
which is stimulated by the situation and the temporary
self in combination may reach much further, bringing
in some of the more general and long-term contours of
the self; and these may bring some sense of unexplained
discord or discomfort with them. C.S.Lewis, in *A Grief
Observed*,[32] describes how the sharp pain of bereavement would be somehow colouring his consciousness
even when his mind was concentrating on other things.
None the less it is possible to have a passing experience
of spaciousness and freedom without all the discords in
ourselves being resolved, especially if we are able for the
moment to live wholeheartedly in the present, taking no
thought for the morrow, as Jesus enjoined. Yet if the
discords are there we will soon run into them again, and

there will be no lasting peace till they have been sorted
out. Dr. Sacks's patients, after their joyful awakening,
usually ran into a period of tribulation:

> A number are broken and fail to survive; others
> endure and are *forged* by their suffering. These
> survivors – the Accommodated – are ... the 'twice-
> born' who after bitter division, physiological and
> social, finally achieve a real reunion, a reconciliation
> of the deepest and stablest kind.[33]

Dr. Sacks is prepared to generalize his conclusions to
apply to all dis-ease, to sin as well as sickness:

> Common to all worlds of disease is the sense of
> pressure, coercion and force; the loss of real spa-
> ciousness and freedom and ease; the loss of poise,
> of infinite readiness, and the contractions, contor-
> tions and postures of illness ... Exorbitance is
> already a first sign of breakdown; it indicates the
> presence of an unmeetable need. Defect, dissat-
> isfaction, underlie exorbitance; a not-enoughness
> somewhere leads to greed and 'too-muchness', to
> a voracity and avidity which *cannot* be met ...
> We are compelled to recognize a precise formal
> analogy (and homology) between pathological pro-
> pensity and sin, and must rank both together as
> ontological peccancy ... Needs and demands which
> cannot be met by reality turn towards substitute
> or compensatory activities, for which they display
> an ever-increasing avidity ... The nature of this
> pathological propensity is essentially extortionate,
> and, if unchecked, must lead to the death of the
> real being ('The wages of sin is death') ... The
> opposite of each exorbitance is a counter-exorbitance
> and patients may be bounced between these ...
> in a frightening paradigm of positive feedback or
> 'anti-control'.[34]

There are some interesting parallels here with Dr. May's
views on addiction and with what we have said earlier
about sin.

It is part of the human condition that even if we achieve
a degree of spaciousness, freedom and health, we are
constantly exposed, through the changes and chances
of life, to new disturbances of this precarious balance,
threats either of disintegration of the self in the face of
the pressures of the world, or of destructive exorbitance
in the self's own attempts to cope. In other words we are
constantly faced with trials and temptations; and to cope
with them we need to have what Dr. Sacks admirably
calls 'infinite readiness', a readiness for change, growth
and readjustment in order to keep the balance and so,
in the terms of our earlier analogy, to ride freely on our
bicycle. Through this process we constantly rediscover
and re-express our true self. In order to do so we have
constant need of grace; and the grace is there if we can
free ourselves enough to heed it. The human spirit can
draw upon extraordinary resources. To give Dr. Sacks the
last word:

> One must allow the possibility of an almost limit-
> less repertoire of functional reorganizations and
> accommodations leading sometimes to unexpected
> and inexplicable resolutions at times when every-
> thing seems lost ... health goes deeper than any
> disease.[35]

Temptation

In its older usage the word temptation does not refer only
to enticement or incitement to do something wrong, it
also means trial or being put to the test. Some scholars
hold that the phrase in the Lord's prayer 'Lead us not
into temptation' is more correctly translated 'Do not
bring us to the test', as in the Anglican Series 3 Service,
the predecessor of the Alternative Service Book. Man is

a purposive creature; we have to want things in order
to live, and it is not easy to think what a life would be
like in which we were not led into any temptations at
all. But our argument so far suggests that, in a stricter
sense, we can use the word to mean all desires or fears
or aversions which are uncontrolled by grace, and are
therefore exorbitant, threatening to take over the self,
and thereby putting us to the test. So it follows that we
should also include all situations, not least situations of
physical suffering, which threaten to test us so far that
we are in danger of being broken or disintegrated. In the
first case the risk is of the whole self being taken over
by the part or parts. This is sin, which is always a loss
of balance and freedom. In the second case the risk is of
the coherence of the self being broken, so that it ceases
to be a whole and ceases to function as a consistent
regulator. This is sickness, breakdown or hardship in
other forms. As I have suggested, sin and sickness (or
hardship) are not so far apart as they seem. In principle
sin only refers to what is under our voluntary control; the
rest is hardship. But in practice such strength as we have
to withstand sickness or hardship may depend in part on
our degree of success on resisting sin. Temptations in
these two forms are forces of evil, negative forces which
damage, and can destroy, the life of human beings.

One of George Herbert's poems is called, in some
editions of his work, 'Tentation' (so spelt). In other
editions the title is 'Affliction'. It may seem strange to
turn to a seventeenth-century poem at this stage. But
human nature is not so variable with time and place as
some modern theorists would suggest; and, in spite of the
initial unfamiliarity of his language and his comparisons,
Herbert goes to the heart of our subject:

Broken in pieces all asunder,
Lord, hunt me not,
A thing forgot,
Once a poore creature, now a wonder,

A wonder tortur'd in the space
Betwixt this world and that of grace.

My thoughts are all a case of knives,
Wounding my heart
With scatter'd smart,
As wat'ring pots give flowers their lives:
Nothing their furie can controll,
While they do wound and prick my soul.

All my attendants are at strife,
Quitting their place
Unto my face;
Nothing performs the task of life:
The elements are let loose to fight.
And while I live trie out their right.

Oh help, my God! let not their plot
Kill them and me,
And also Thee,
Who art my life: dissolve the knot,
As the sunne scatters by his light
All the rebellions of the night.

Then shall those powers which work for grief
Enter Thy pay,
And day by day
Labour Thy praise and my relief;
With care and courage building me
Till I reach heav'n, and, much more, Thee.

Herbert, who died of tuberculosis at thirty-nine, suffered
years of ill health. A man of great attainments who
was also of noble birth, he faced the enticements and
ambitions of life at court, and wrote about the difficulties
they caused him. He also suffered, as this poem and many
others show, the trials of psychological and spiritual
conflict. When he was on his deathbed, as reported
by Izaak Walton, he sent the manuscript of his poems
to his friend Nicholas Ferrar of Little Gidding, with a

message that he would find in it 'a picture of the many
spiritual conflicts that have past betwixt God and my
soul, before I could subject mine to the will of Jesus
my Master: in whose service I have now found perfect
freedom'. His poems reflect, with remarkable liveliness,
intimacy and honesty, the sufferings and joys of the
never-ending process of the purification of conscience
through prayer. In 'Tentation' we see him torn between
the two centres of this world and grace, suffering the
agonies of persecuting, perhaps remorseful, thoughts, so
disintegrated that his 'attendants' (whom I take to be
his natural talents and capacities) have deserted him,
while the elements – the separate parts of him – 'trie out
their right' and attempt to take over his soul. He rightly
sees all these as 'rebellions' against his God and king,
to whom he now turns. And his prayer is not for their
destruction but for their integration, so that the powers
which work for grief can enter the Lord's service, 'with
care and courage building me, till I reach heav'n', the
state of grace and freedom, 'and, much more, Thee.' In
finding his true self he finds his God.

The poems of George Herbert can tell us a great deal
about the nature of the struggle against temptation,
which is the struggle against evil. This is sometimes
described as spiritual warfare and seen very much in
terms of a battle against demons or Satan himself,
that is, against evil in personified form. The test of
being a person, I suggested earlier, is possessing an
independent will. In the case of our more straightforward trials and temptations we recognize desires or
fears within ourselves which we may wish to combat,
but which we still know to be very much our own. It
is a matter of our own will in conflict with our own
'elements' or desires. Sometimes however the situation is
more complex. The dominating desire or fear in question
gathers other elements round itself in a complex pattern
– mostly below the level of consciousness – and seems
to represent an alternative whole, an alternative will,

ready to take over the self. It is not wrong to characterize such an entity as a demon. Jung describes demons as 'autonomous complexes' within the self. They are indeed evil, for their effect is entirely negative, they bring with them sin, sickness, destruction for the natural being; they cannot stand independently as something positive; they are like a whirlpool within the self.

In an extreme case a person's own will and pattern of integration can be shattered and his mind and body taken over and possessed by such an autonomous complex. The old structure of the anticipating self is broken up and a new set of stories affecting its broadest and most long-term contours is put in place, while the old ones are pushed into unconsciousness. 'Men loved darkness because their deeds were evil.' As we justify and rationalize our evil deeds with new stories we descend a spiral into the dark. The mind eventually goes over to a new centre, but not to a centre of grace, rather to a new central idea of the self. This may come from within, taking the form either of some dominating pride or ambition or, paradoxically, of some dominating depressive self-denigration. Alternatively it may come from without, usually through the dispossession of the individual and his total identification with some human leader or ideology, an identification which produces bondage and idolatry.

Depression, as this implies, can itself be understood as a form of autonomous complex. It seems to grow out of a fear of rejection or abandonment, usually rooted in experiences of the earliest weeks or months of babyhood. The fear of rejection develops into an acceptance of rejection: we accept that we are of no value or importance, not only in the eyes of other people, but in our own eyes, and often in God's eyes too. This leads to great anger (usually bottled up and repressed out of consciousness) and to great misery. We are trapped and imprisoned, nothing interests us, making any decision is purgatory. Yet to begin with, as I have suggested, we seem to turn to depression as a way of deadening pain. Then it can become an addiction. An experience of humiliation or rejection in adult life can bring it back in a flood which overwhelms our sense of proportion and our sense of reality. There is no question here of attaching blame to the unfortunate sufferer. Depression is not something we can snap out of; it cannot be fought with the muscular will. We can only grow out of it gradually by identifying where it comes from, seeing that the self it creates and the world it creates are *illusions*, then recognizing and growing back into the true, free self and the real world.[36]

Either way, whether the autonomous complex grows from within or without, it is important to recognize that this evil phantasm remains a negative, destructive force, it does not stand as a positive opposite, creating an alternative world. A person possessed can sometimes have magnetic powers as a leader and can create the looming structures of an evil kingdom. But in the end they are always illusory, because in turning away from grace we turn away from the means of truth and begin to live in a fantasy world. We twist our understanding of reality to match our own idolatry. We cut ourselves off from truth, therefore from God, therefore in the end from other people. We begin to live with ghosts, like Shakespeare's Richard III in his last hours, or Stalin near his end, with the phantoms of the 'doctors' plot'. The most accurate definition of hell is being cut off from God. For Milton's Satan 'Which way I fly is Hell; myself am Hell.'

The human condition is such that there is a great deal of evil in ourselves and in the world, perhaps as the counterpart of a still more immense potential for growing into good. Evil penetrates the systems, organizations and structures of the world, and this is how I understand St.Paul's reference in the Epistle to the Colossians to the disarming by Christ of the 'principalities and powers'. We are constantly tempted, it is evil that tempts us, and this evil often takes the personal form of a will to evil, not only in the individual members of the human race, but in its collective structures. These can develop a collective will which is more than the will of any one individual. But if we regard evil in such a form as personal or demonic, we need to be extremely cautious over setting up a Satan who is almost a counterpart of Christ, and thus falling into a heretical dualism. The Satan of the Book of Job is an instrument of God, however hard this may be to understand, not a towering potential rival, like the Satan of Milton or Satan the great dragon of the Book of Revelation. I think it is safer, if we wish to talk in terms of Satan, to use the Job image rather than the Revelation image. But on the whole, while in no way denying the reality of these evil forces, I prefer to use the psychological language of autonomous complexes or paranoid belief systems, or the language of St John and St Paul, based on the images of light and darkness, life and death, rather than the language of demons.

In doing so it may be said that I beg the question of whether these demons are small transparent entities which float about and can move into people and out of them again. Frankly I can't myself think of them in that way. I am sure that mental complexes can be communicated from one person to another, not only through words and gestures but also to some extent in more direct ways which are still little understood. They can possess crowds and organizations, which are both in different ways communication systems. I would also accept that there may possibly be some circumstances in which a sort of vortex of experience from the past can be transmitted to a living human being. For the past is part of reality, even when it is unrecorded and inaccessible to us and some sort of transmission from the past is a far more plausible explanation of certain curious reported phenomena than theories of reincarnation or the wheel of rebirth. But in all these areas our understanding is extremely limited. Much depends on the language and metaphors we use, and we need to be both humble and cautious in our assertions.

Healing

Healing is a process of being set free from our hang-ups, our sin, our sickness, so that we can grow into the maturity of our true selves. We are not, in this life, cured of the human condition. We are not spared from conflict, injustice, misfortune, physical suffering, old age and death. If we are truly healed, we may in fact face a harder life, and may, as Jesus implied, be persecuted for righteousness' sake. But healing will give us the strength to cope; and sometimes it may set us free from sickness not only of the mind or spirit, but also of the body.

Truth is the great healer; and the healing process begins with facing the truth, or in religious terms *confession*. This does not require beating of the breast or cultivated sorrow, it requires humility; and this in turn is not a grovelling self-abasement, but rather the simplicity and directness of mind that will register the truth. It has little to do with listing the occasions on which we have broken moral rules or done things of which we are ashamed. It has much more to do with understanding and facing the reasons why we did these things, and perhaps more still with a deeper understanding of the stories we tell ourselves, of our wider motivations and the ways in which we conceal them from ourselves and others. Confession or self-examination in this sense is a long and difficult process, and never fully completed. Much of the work of a counsellor or psychotherapist is a matter of helping people to understand themselves better, to recognize their excuses and defences for what they are, and so to make themselves vulnerable to the cleansing blade of truth. Much thought has been given in recent decades by psychoanalysts and others to this search for truth and the recognition of its negative – lies and self-deception. The essential work, however, has to

be done by the client, or, better said, by the Spirit of
Truth working within the client. For, as Dr. Sacks wisely
put it, health goes deeper than any disease. There is a
propensity and potential for wholeness in each one of us,
which begins with the need for truth. The writer of Psalm
51 expresses this need, together with his assurance that
God will help:

> But lo, thou requirest truth in the inward parts:
>   and shalt make me to understand wisdom
>   secretly . . .
> Thou shalt make me hear of joy and gladness: that
>   the bones that thou hast broken may rejoice . . .
> Make me a clean heart. O God: and renew a right
>   spirit within me . . .
> O give me the comfort of thy help again: and stablish
>   me with thy free spirit.

And once again a poem of George Herbert goes to the
heart of the matter. This one is entitled 'Confession'.
As in many poems of his time, the writer works out
the implications of a central image or 'conceit'. In this
case he takes the image of the human heart which puts
up defences in the form of closets, chests and boxes,
one within the other, to ward off pain, but succeeds
only in shutting in its afflictions and fencing out the
healing truth.

>   O what a cunning guest
> Is this same grief! within my heart I made
>   Closets, and in them many a chest;
>   And like a master of my trade,
> In those chests, boxes; in each box a till,
> Yet Grief knows all, and enters when he will.
>
>   No scrue, no piercer can
> Into a piece of timber worke and winde
>   As God's afflictions into man,

When He a torture hath design'd;
They are too subtill for the subt'llest hearts,
And fall like rheumes upon the tendrest parts.

      We are the earth; and they
Like moles within us, heave and cast about;
      And till they foot and clutch their prey,
         They never cool, much lesse give out.
No smith can make such locks but they have keyes
Closets are halls to them, and hearts high-wayes.

        Onely an open breast
Doth shut them out, so that they cannot enter;
      Or if they enter, cannot rest,
        But quickly seek some new adventure:
Smooth open hearts no fastning have; but fiction
Doth give a hold and handle to affliction.

      Wherefore my faults and sinnes,
Lord, I acknowledge; take thy plagues away:
      For since confession pardon winnes,
        I challenge here the brightest day,
The clearest diamond; let them do their best,
They shall be thick and cloudie to my breast.

After facing the truth we come to *repentance*, otherwise
penitence. This, like confession, is not a matter of beating
your breast. It means turning to God. In secular or
Jungian terms it means going over to a new centre and
so establishing a new, free pattern of coherence. Turning
to God, or going over to a new centre, however, inevitably
means turning away from the old self, rejecting old values
and priorities. This cannot be achieved without sacrifice
and pain; and sometimes the emotional impact can be
shattering. Christians are all too liable to say glibly such
words as 'we offer you our souls and bodies to be a living
sacrifice' without any clear awareness of how much they
are saying.

True repentance involves a careful, explicit recognition

and rejection of the things from which we are turning away; and this can bring us not only sadness over time ill-spent and harm done to others, but also, it must be acknowledged, a painful sense of bereavement over the loss of the old self and the addictions or attachments that we are giving up. There is much of human nature in St Augustine's youthful prayer: 'Give me chastity and continence, but not yet.' Furthermore, although sorrow over our past failings can be useful in helping us to reinforce our determination to turn to God or to a new and truer centre for our lives, it can be morbidly destructive if it leads us to self-hatred and depression. For essentially, repentance is a liberation and an occasion for the joy and gladness of the psalmist, even though there may be some immediate withdrawal symptoms. In any event we should not allow ourselves to be deceived into thinking how meritorious our painful emotions are. That way we end by using them to conceal from ourselves how incomplete our repentance really is.

The hard part comes when repentance brings home to us the harm we have done to other people. If it is a true repentance it will lead us to want to make *reparation* so far as we can; and making reparation is therefore an intrinsic element in the process of healing. But often it is impossible to undo what we have done, or to make good what we have left undone, and then we find ourselves plunged into *remorse*, which can be perhaps the most bitter of all the emotions of which humans are capable. We sometimes try to suppress remorse and bury it into unconsciousness. This can be fatal, since it festers on unseen, souring our lives and eventually breaking out in disguised and dangerous ways. All we can truly do with remorse is to be open to it and accept it, to make ourselves vulnerable to it, and let it burn itself through. This process takes time, but it does come to an end. Only in this way can we be purged and eventually set free. If we have genuinely faced our sin, forgiveness is already there, even as we work through the purgatory of remorse. Yet again it is important that we should not attempt to cultivate remorse, or deceive ourselves into thinking that we acquire some sort of merit through it.

The imposition of *penances* on people who have confessed their sins, which is one of the traditional practices of the Church, is in principle a way of enabling them to work through their remorse by, as it were, externalizing it. Psychologically it corresponds to a deep-rooted human sentiment that wrong should be punished and can thereby in some sense be expiated. But the practice is open to abuse in two ways. First it can encourage the idea that it is the penance, the hair shirt, which puts one right with God, rather than the transformation of the self which it may or may not facilitate: in theological terms it can encourage the idea of justification by works. Secondly it can encourage a morbid wallowing in guilt, when the forgiveness is already there if we will only accept it. We should not suppress or avoid remorse, but neither should we seek it out. In recent years it has become customary, in those Christian traditions which make use of formal, sacramental confession, for the confessor to propose as a penance no more than the reading of a psalm or the praying of a collect, perhaps over a certain time; and this seems to me the right and appropriate course.

Guilt is the emotional accompaniment of our awareness of sin. It is the emotion that is stirred in us by the resonance of a sinful act that we have committed or that we have in mind. It is what we feel when we put the old self first rather than the new, when we let some desire, fear, pride or ambition become exorbitant and so claim our first allegiance. It is what we feel when we fall off the bicycle, the bad conscience which hits us when we adopt, or think of adopting, a plan or role that conflicts with the long-term stories and ideal roles of the anticipating self. It can include a sense of *shame*, which is the unpleasant emotion we experience when we are seen by others to be doing something that does not match the stories we have told them.

To put it another way, sin is failure to meet our responsibility and use our freedom. Guilt is the emotion which points us towards our sin and forces us to acknowledge it, instead of burying it. Once the sin is fully acknowledged, guilt has no further rightful part to play. Forgiveness is there to meet us and if we can accept it the guilt turns to liberation, either directly or, where necessary, in and through our experiences of reparation or remorse. If we refuse to accept the forgiveness and go on belabouring ourselves (which unfortunately is not a rare phenomenon) we are in fact committing a further sin, growing out of fear or pride or both, as we try to justify ourselves by grovellings and protestations instead of accepting God's grace.

The capacity to feel guilt is essential to health; a person who cannot feel guilt is a psychopath and a danger to society. But, as we saw when we considered the nature of conscience, the anticipating self is a confused and ramshackle structure, especially in those reaches which are inaccessible to consciousness. Guilt can be inappropriate when it reflects the patterns of a primitive, childish super-ego, rather than the honest judgments of an adult. On the other hand it can be highly appropriate when we do something which subconsciously we know in our heart of hearts is wrong, while in consciousness we deceive ourselves into thinking it is not. How, then, do you tell the difference between the two cases? The answer can only be through self-knowledge, otherwise the purification of conscience:

> Smooth open hearts no fastning have; but fiction
> Doth give a hold and handle to affliction.

There is no substitute for self-knowledge, whether we approach it through psychological techniques or the prayer of confession or both. And the core of the process is

to recognize the 'fictions', the defences against the truth,
which we all put up in order to protect our old selves from
change. These are the denials, the repressions, the projections, the projective identifications, the introjections,
the displacements, the avoidances, the withdrawals and
so on with which the counsellor and the psychotherapist
concern themselves. George Herbert did not use this
sort of language; but, writing three centuries before the
Freudian revolution, he understood very well in his own
fashion the nature of such defences.

Herbert is very ready to recognize his own sinfulness
and to accept blame for it. There are several poems on
this theme ('Sinne's Round' is a particularly powerful
one). But it is interesting that he speaks of 'God's
afflictions'. He takes responsibility for what is his, but
not for that which is beyond his control: and in the end
he loves and trusts his God, whom he can even address
in a playful way. This is 'Bitter-Sweet':

> Ah, my deare angrie Lord,
> Since Thou dost love, yet strike,
> Cast down, yet help afford;
> Sure I will do the like.
>
> I will complain yet praise,
> I will bewail, approve;
> And all my sowre-sweet dayes
> I will lament, and love.

There is a confidence and truthfulness about Herbert's
relationship with his God, even in his poems of deepest
affliction, which is not often to be found. In the Christian
understanding God is the God of mercy and love; but all
too often Christians think of him as the God of wrath,
blame and judgment. They know in theory that God is
love, but in practice they are mistrustful; they fear him
more than they love him; and that is one reason why
they find it difficult to be really truthful with him and
themselves.

Justice

There is a good deal in the Bible that can be used to reinforce the idea of a God who creates humans wretched and then gives them hell. But there is any amount more to show that this is not the true understanding. We learn that the beginning of wisdom is to fear the Lord; and this is true in the sense that we must, at our peril, recognize with awe that overwhelming and mysterious reality within which we all live and move and have our being: 'I am that I am'. But in the Book of the Wisdom of Solomon in the Apocrypha it is said of wisdom, still more profoundly, that 'her very true beginning is the desire of discipline; and the care [the concern] of discipline is love'. A loving discipline is there to set you free, not to hold you down. It represents the coming of God's kingdom. Christians often need to learn that you can't really love God until you trust him; and you can't trust him if you are afraid of him. Being afraid is not the same thing as being in awe of him. The combination of awe and the recognition of mystery with trust and love is the mark of true worship. George Herbert again, using the image of Justice with her scales:

'O dreadfull justice, what a fright and terrour
    Wast thou of old,
    When Sinne and Errour
Did show and shape thy looks to me,
And through their glasse discolour thee!
He that did but look up was proud and bold.

The dishes of thy balance seem'd to gape
    Like two great pits;
    The beam and 'scape
Did like some tort'ring engine show:
Thy hand above did burn and glow,
Daunting the stoutest hearts, the proudest wits.

But now that Christ's pure vail presents the sight,

I see no fears:
Thy hand is white,
Thy scales like buckets, which attend
And interchangeably descend,
Lifting to heaven from this well of tears.

For where before thou still didst call on me,
Now I still touch
And harp on thee;
God's promises have made thee mine:
Why should I justice now decline?
Against me there is none, but for me much.

It is not Christians only who suffer from inappropriate guilt, deriving ultimately from the harshness of
a primitive super-ego; it is a very common affliction
among all sorts of people. And we will not be set free
from it by denying sin and guilt altogether, as humanists
sometimes try to do, especially when they are influenced
by the determinism of some strands of scientific thinking,
or by the social determinism of a Marxist analysis.
That usually results in projecting the guilt upon others,
who become the scapegoats for our own bad conscience.
Inappropriate guilt can only be healed by purifying our
conscience, recognizing both the extent of our freedom
and its limits, and taking responsibility for what is ours.
(Those who cannot feel a responsibility to God can still, if
they are people of good will, accept a responsibility to the
rest of humanity for the way they conduct their lives.)

The question can be asked whether, if we are not faced
with a punishing God, there is any particular need to
accept responsibility at all. Why should we bother to
be good? Although God does not seek to punish us,
he does give us free will and thereby gives us the
opportunity to make our own freely creative contribution
to the continuing work of building the kingdom; but the
converse of this is that if we do not use the opportunity,
if we do not turn to him, we become gradually alienated

from him and so cut off from reality. The punishment
is real, but we create it for ourselves. The writer of
the fourth gospel tells us that God sent his Son into
the world not to condemn it but to save it; but he goes
on: 'He who believes in him is not condemned; he who
does not believe is condemned already.'[37] In the words of
the biblical scholar C.H. Dodd, 'The wrath of God . . ., as
seen in actual operation, consists in leaving sinful human
nature to stew in its own juice'. If you have ever had
experience of people locked by their pride into a belief
system that twists the whole world to justify their own
self-image, you will know the accuracy of that remark.
As I believe D.H. Lawrence wrote somewhere:

> It is a fearful thing to fall
> Into the hands of the living God;
> But it is a far, far more fearful thing
> To fall out of the hands of the living God.

God apparently does not intervene in such cases, as
that would be to interfere with human free will; but he
does not directly inflict punishment on sinners. Indeed I
believe he suffers when they suffer. God's justice is not
to be separated from his mercy and his love; they are all
poured out from the same fountain.[38]

It is hardly within the scope of this book to discuss the
after-life, but I do not want to shirk the questions that
arise in this connexion. Ought we to be good simply in
order to avoid eternal torment? I doubt if that is a real
option. I think it is the wrong question, because if we
do something out of fear, we are not doing it freely and
we are not in the kingdom anyway. 'Fear has to do with
punishment, and he who fears is not perfected in love.'[39]
If we are truly walking in the Spirit we act in freedom
and out of love; we are co-operating in the kingdom. As a
matter of faith I believe it is profoundly, metaphysically,
important that we should do so, and thereby make good
use of our lives. It was for this reason that God sent

his Son into the world. In so far as we do so, we have
freedom in this life, and, in some manner beyond human
grasp, after our death the life we have lived, that is sown
perishable in the earth, is raised imperishable, in total
transformation, into a new being. In the process the
evil in our lives, like the husk of the grain of wheat,
is shed and goes back into the dust. Perhaps there are
some people, self-condemned, whose lives are so sharply
turned away from God that in the end there is only husk
and dust left, there is nothing that God can use. But I
hope not. In the words of St Paul, speaking of Christ as
the second Adam:

> As was the man of dust, so are those who are of the
> dust; and as is the man of heaven, so are those who
> are of heaven. Just as we have borne the image of
> the man of dust, we shall also bear the image of the
> man of heaven.[40]

It is not part of my purpose here to press particular views
about the after-life. The point that I do want to press
home is the simple good news that *forgiveness* is there
for all of us, Jew or Gentile, male or female, Christian
or agnostic or anything else, all the time. Forgiveness
means being set free from the burden of sin, addiction and
guilt and so being healed. All we have to do is to face the
truth, to turn to God and to turn away from our old self.
In the words of the psalmist which I quoted earlier, 'O
taste and see how gracious the Lord is.' The forgiveness
is there already, like that of the father running to meet
his prodigal son in the most wonderful of all parables.
The grace is there – 'prevenient grace' coming ahead of
us – through which we can steer our lives in obedience
and perfect freedom. It is not easy to steer by grace. We
will constantly fail. But when we fail, the love of God is
always there, ready to pick us up and dust us off and set
us on our way again. 'We love', says St. John, 'because
he first loved us.'

Finally, what of those who cannot accept the Christian language I have been using? I suggest that they might think in terms, first, of accepting the responsibility for their lives which goes with human free will; secondly of finding and going over to a new centre for the self, breaking with past patterns and addictions, and so finding freedom and release from guilt; and thirdly of recognizing that they can always turn back for renewal to their centre of balance, truth, freedom and love. In my understanding, where there is true self-giving love, there is God, even if he is not known by name.

CHAPTER FIVE

LOVING AND BEING LOVED

Truth in Relationships

In all relationships truth is the ultimate healer; but truthfulness used as a blunderbuss does not serve the truth: it simply drives up the barriers to communication – fear and anger. So how and when does truth serve the purposes of love? And when and how does love tell the truth?

In considering these questions my starting point will be the perceptive analysis of interpersonal relationships made by the social psychologist Erving Goffman in his well-known book, *The Presentation of the Self in Everyday Life*. There is no scope in this context for an extended account of his analysis, but I will begin from his basic view of what happens when a person encounters others. What happens first, he suggests, is that they have to arrive at a common definition of the situation:

> When an individual appears before others, he knowingly and unwittingly projects a definition of the situation of which a conception of himself is an important part.[1]

This conception or account of himself (or herself) is what I have called a presentational role, the story which he tells others in this situation. This is a part of the story which he tells *himself* in this situation, a part of the temporary or responding self which constitutes Me-Here-Now. But it is only a part; the outer, presentational story seldom reflects the inner story exactly or completely. Goffman emphasizes that what the individual says or does will have a 'promissory' character, it will give people reason to expect him to behave in certain ways. The others are likely to find that they have to accept the individual's version of himself if they are to co-operate together. Meanwhile they, by their responses, also project definitions of the situation and accompanying conceptions of themselves:

> Ordinarily the definitions projected by the several different participants are sufficiently attuned to one another so that open contradictions do not occur ... Each participant is expected to suppress his immediate, heartfelt feelings, conveying a view of the situation which he feels the others will be able to find at least temporarily acceptable ... Each participant is allowed to establish his tentative official role regarding matters which are vital to him ... e.g. the rationalizations and justifications by which he accounts for his past activity. In exchange ... he remains silent or non-committal on matters important to others but not immediately important to him ... Together the participants contribute to a single overall definition of the situation which involves not so much a real agreement as to what exists, but rather a real agreement as to what claims concerning what issues will be temporarily honoured.[2]

This abbreviated version does little justice to the subtlety of Goffman's analysis, and inevitably it lacks the acutely observed case-stories with which he supports it. But what he is doing is to point out some of the features of what is happening under our noses all the time, without our being conscious of it, whenever we deal with other people. It is a practical necessity of life for us to co-operate

with one another, and so to find the common ground
required for our co-operation, without allowing other
aspects of ourselves to get in the way. Goffman suggests
that at the core of every encounter between humans is
a set of stories which are self-projections. These are
restricted to aspects of the person which are relevant to
the situation as that person perceives it. Between them
they help to define the values – otherwise the priorities of
purpose – which are to be jointly applied in the situation
as the people concerned work together to identify and
achieve some objective that they have in common. Sin-
cerity, consistency, and hence truth, are required from
the participants, but only within this restricted frame
of reference. In any case the ultimate truth 'as to what
exists' is not at stake, only a provisional agreement as to
what is to be accepted for immediate practical purposes.
Questions are carefully not asked about each individual's
deeper 'rationalizations and justifications'.

Any analysis in abstract terms of such a process
inevitably sounds ponderous, not least because much
of the communication involved takes place not through
words in formed sentences, but through exclamations,
smiles, gestures, inflexions, tones of voice and 'body
language' of all kinds. This communication is carried
on almost entirely without conscious deliberation by the
communicator, whose mind is on the general intention,
not the means he or she is using. Consider what happens
when I go up to an assistant in a bookshop to make an
enquiry about a book, and eventually to buy it. I am in
the presenting role of customer and the assistant has
no need to know anything more about me. The physical
surroundings of the bookshop are themselves sufficient
to define our two presenting roles in nearly all the detail
that is necessary. When I go up to the assistant with
a smile and she responds, we have already virtually
defined together a situation concerned with locating and
buying a book. The assistant may be preoccupied with
some domestic problem of her own, but, if so, she will

keep these thoughts to herself, while we get on with concluding the deal. If I make a mistake and go up to another customer, thinking she is the shop assistant, confusion and embarrassment will follow. It is partly to avoid such misunderstandings that a good deal of effort often goes into what Goffman calls 'supportive interchanges', 'remedial interchanges' (such as will be necessary when there has been a mistake of this kind) and other small acts of 'interpersonal ritual', through which people help each other to sustain, repair and reinforce their presentational roles.[3] For in general we are careful not to pull each other's acts to pieces so long as any sort of fruitful co-operative interaction is still in view.

A passing negotiation in a bookshop is one thing. But a longer-term relationship which involves frequent interactions in a variety of situations – as for example one between friends, or working colleagues, or relatives, or marriage partners – is something quite different. In the more transitory relationships, as we have seen, our commitment to each other is limited to the matter in hand, and the accounts we give of ourselves are correspondingly angled and foreshortened; we do not expect to pry into each other's deeper self-justifications. But when it comes to a longer-term relationship we are not satisfied with being offered a series of different and sometimes discrepant stories. Our own commitment is no longer transitory, and so we feel we have a right to know how these various stories hang together, what is the 'real' self underlying and linking them. Usually an individual will meet this claim by offering a further story, which gives an account of the deeper-lying plans and roles of his or her anticipating self. With the mutual exchange of such deeper presentations a foundation is laid for a relationship of greater understanding, and so of greater mutual trust and commitment.

However it is not easy to build deeper relationships of this kind. The more you tell, the more you make yourself vulnerable. As we saw earlier, the plans and roles which build up an individual's anticipating self are also that individual's defences. If I tell you about my deeper fears, plans, self-justifications and ambitions, I expose a lot of surface; and if you criticize or disparage or ridicule these stories, or show them to be based on delusions, you threaten that which holds me together – not only my fragile self-esteem, but my very self. Consequently I will not do it unless I feel I can trust you. And I can only trust you if you assure me, not once but repeatedly, of your acceptance of me and my stories, and if you reciprocate by telling me corresponding stories about your own deeper fears, plans, self-justifications and ambitions, so that you make yourself equally vulnerable to me. The more we open ourselves to each other, the greater is our need for supportive and remedial interchanges and interpersonal ritual, in order to maintain what has become a deeper and more emotionally sensitive relationship.

Generally even the more comprehensive accounts that people give of themselves in longer-term relationships are still not the whole truth. They may have peeled off some layers of the onion, but other layers still remain, even when they are trying to be honest. No account ever quite gets down to the naked self. In some cases people hold back deliberately, either to preserve their freedom of manoeuvre, or because the unvarnished truth would be unacceptable to their partners, or because the relationship has its recognized boundaries anyway. But often they cling to what may feel like more presentable versions of themselves as a defence against being forced to bring out plans and motivations of which they are largely unaware because they have been repressed into unconsciousness.

In such a case if the partner is prepared to go along with the cover story in ignorance, no immediate tension may result, though the relationship will be less than it could be. But generally the partner is consciously dissatisfied, and has at least an inkling of the reason why; on the whole we have sharper eyes for others' self-deceptions than for our own. And it can be intolerable in a relationship such as a marriage to be asked to commit yourself to your partner's act rather than to the true person. Nothing is more destructive of love than a sense of falsity in the situation. But, conversely, a situation in which both partners understand their own selves at some depth and are able to be truly open with each other, trusting themselves to each other, can be a great strength and blessing in people's lives. For a relationship of mutual openness, mutual commitment, mutual vulnerability, mutual trust and mutual identification is a relationship of love.

It is on this understanding of love that I propose to base my approach to all issues concerning human relationships. As I see it, all relationships are to do with co-operation in living. Some are quite limited in their scope and involve only limited self-commitment; but, even so, truthfulness and openness within the recognized boundaries of the relationship are essential if co-operation is to be effective. Beyond this it is also essential for those concerned to be able to support each other in their respective presenting roles, observing the courtesies of interpersonal ritual, and thereby giving honour and consideration to the human being behind the role. To do this is to identify with the other in common humanity. Even in a passing transaction with a shop assistant the courtesies of the smile and the thank-you are important, while rudeness on either side can be destructive; rudeness implies contempt. In the case of deeper and longer-term relationships the need for truthfulness and for courtesy and consideration is all the greater, and sometimes much more difficult to achieve. For the deeper the relationship and the greater the self-commitment, the greater the extent to which we identify ourselves with the other and so put our own selves at risk. In a true sense the word identification can be taken as a litmus test for love. If I love my child, then if the child is in pain then I too suffer, and if the child is happy then I too rejoice. If there is no such identification, my love is false.

Falling in Love

There is a distinction to be drawn between the experience of 'falling in love' or 'being in love', as these phrases are commonly used, and the enduring love which is not so much an experience as an integrated aspect of the person. This is broadly the distinction drawn in Greek between *eros* and St Paul's word *agape*. The latter used to be translated as charity, but charity now has a different meaning. Lovingkindness comes closer, since the root meaning of 'kind' reflects kinship or identification. But in modern English we cannot escape from using the word love in both senses, and this even has its advantages, since it prevents us from sharpening the distinction when in fact there is an overlap. There is a sexual component to being in love which is essential to its meaning, though it is not the whole of it. Similarly there can be a sexual component in what I distinguish as enduring love, but there does not have to be; love in this sense has a much broader meaning and can include love between parents and children, between other relatives and between friends, indeed even a sense of identification with all human-kind.

Psychologically the core of the process of falling in love seems to be the projection of some part of the self upon the other person. Projection is one of the more complex of the ways in which the mind adapts to reality, and as a mechanism it goes much wider than the process of falling in love. It may therefore be helpful to begin with a few general comments on this mechanism.

Broadly those strands of our being which are repressed into the unconscious are those which cannot easily be reconciled with the conscious layers of the anticipating self, or at least could not be so reconciled at the time when they were repressed. To recall some points made in Chapter One, these strands represent the obverse of those sides of us which are most developed and differentiated; and together they form what Jung called the Shadow. The elements of the Shadow are generally undeveloped and somewhat primitive, and often include tendencies towards anger, aggression, lust and anti-social behaviour which in childhood met with disapproval from parent figures, and later continue to be disapproved by the internalized parent figures of the super-ego. As Dr. Anthony Storr has said, 'It is a remarkable and interesting fact that parts of the personality which have been disowned in childhood remain infantile.'[4] Nevertheless they are still part of the individual and there is pressure for them to find expression in some disguised form. They usually do this either in the form of symptoms, such as phobias or obsessive rituals, or as projections. We often project upon other people the things we dislike and do not want to admit about ourselves. We attribute to them motives and intentions which are not in fact theirs but (secretly) ours; and in extreme cases this can lead to paranoid fantasies of persecution.

It is also possible for us to project positive qualities upon other people, perhaps particularly those with whom we feel we can identify. Such are the heroes and heroines – the other children, teachers, pop stars, sports personalities, film stars and others – with whom young people identify themselves at different stages as they grow up. Often these stars in the adolescent firmament are invested with a fascination and a magic which it is hard for others to understand; and Dr. Storr's explanation is that they reflect parts of the individual's own personality which are undeveloped, latent, and therefore potential rather than actual. As he puts it, these parts of the adolescent individual may be set in vibration by the impact of personalities with the same frequency. The individual falls in love, as it were, with his or her

own latent potentialities.[5] Projection in this form is an
important part of the process of growing up and one of the
main ways in which latent potentialities are discovered
and brought out.

Growing out of this form of projection, yet crucially
different from it, is the true process of falling in love,
in which sexual desire is a central and explicit component. It was Freud who first brought us to recognize
that there is an element of femininity in every man
and an element of masculinity in every woman. Jung
described these 'contrasexual' elements as the *anima*
in a man and the *animus* in a woman. Because of
their contrasexual nature these elements are inevitably
difficult to reconcile with the main structures of the
anticipating self, and they tend in consequence to be
repressed into unconsciousness, and to share the naivety
and undeveloped character of much that forms part of the
Shadow. Jung, however, took the view that they are not
in fact part of the Shadow, they form a separate strand
or layer in the structure of the self. When in dreams
or fantasies we personify the Shadow as an expression
of the archetype, to use Jung's terminology, it always
emerges as a person of the same sex as the dreamer.
When a man dreams of an anima figure, however, it is
almost invariably female; and conversely when a woman
dreams of an animus figure, it is almost always male.
(Exceptions may reflect failures at an earlier stage in
the establishment of sexual identity.) For Jung anima
and animus, representing the 'soul image', are independent archetypes, that is, independent elements of the
underlying structure of the psyche common respectively
to all male and all female human beings. Falling in
love is a process of projecting the anima or animus
upon the person whom one loves. As P.W. Martin has
described it:

> In actual life a man normally encounters the anima
> first in the form of a projection. There is a sudden

overwhelming 'falling in love' and for a while nothing else in the world matters. The woman on whom the projection is cast becomes for him no creature of flesh and blood, but a divinity, an enchantment. From her he expects everything. She knows the Great Secret, she holds the key to life. The thought of separation is impossible; existence would be meaningless without her. They have met in some previous life, they have known and been fated for one another throughout the ages. A special light pervades the whole landscape, illumining especially the woman on whom this projection from the unconscious has fallen ... So long as the projection lasts, the man is held by a completely irrational attachment ... for she has upon her an essential part of his inmost being.[6]

This is perhaps an extreme case, but many cases are pretty extreme, and we can easily recognize what Martin is describing. The love songs of every generation make the enchantment known:

Then let the seas run dry, sweetheart,
The rocks melt with the sun,
Yet here will I stay, nor ever from thee part,
Till all my days are done, my dear,
Till all my days are done.

As Dr. Storr has said: 'To be in love ... is inadequately explained in terms only of the need for genital satisfaction ... no experience is more magical ... Lovers feel as if they were made for each other; as if no one else could possibly fulfil their need; as if they themselves were *incomplete* without the other person.' And he adds: 'The mutual projection ... seems to indicate a search for completeness, a reaching out after wholeness, a union between conscious and unconscious ... The image which each projects upon the other exhibits the psychological as well as the anatomical attributes which distinguish the sexes.'[7] Conventional psychological ideals of masculinity and femininity vary, he says, from one culture to another, but such ideals exist in some form in every culture.

Unfortunately such love is not always returned, and the pangs of unrequited love are as acute as any of which humans are capable. But, except in pathological cases, they do not last indefinitely; and the same, alas, is true even of the ecstasies of fully requited love. Yet 'alas' is too glib a word to use. In a true marriage the projections are gradually withdrawn, and they have to be withdrawn if the marriage is to be founded on the rock of reality. It is of great importance that the element of idealization and illusion should be replaced before too long by a true understanding, respect and love for the real person (though the ecstasies may still perhaps be recaptured from time to time, particularly in sexual union). And in this process the overwhelming nature of the experience of falling in love can serve a most valuable purpose in helping to break down many of the layers of defences with which we surround ourselves. In this fashion it can pave the way for the 'marriage of true minds' which in the end is an even greater, more permanent blessing than the uncertain glory of being in love. It is characteristic of two young people in love that they spend innumerable hours talking to each other about themselves, or, if separated, writing love letters to each other. Through this process both tend to give each other long and intimate, even if selective, accounts of their younger days, the experiences of their lives, their parents, their families, their friends, their schooldays, even their previous love affairs. All this serves the purpose of peeling off layers of the onion of the self, so that the relationship comes to be grounded more and more on truth rather than on mutual projections of the anima and animus. It is

a way of beginning to build a relationship of enduring love.

Obstacles to Loving (1): Baggage from the Past

A passionate experience of being in love may give a flying
start to a potential marital relationship. But as the projections come to be withdrawn, and disillusioning reality
begins to come through, a major obstacle to enduring love
can make itself felt, namely the tendency to cling to past
idealizations of the other, which then themselves become
defences of the self. This is ultimately a clinging to an
illusory part of oneself, a reluctance not merely to face
reality, but also to give oneself freely to the real other.
True loving involves a self-giving which is a genuine
sacrifice of the old self, a dying in order to live. Both
lovers have to be ready to change and adjust to each
other in order to build a relationship which is greater
than either of them individually, and transcends them
both. The illusion that the relationship was 'made in
heaven' and they are specially designed for one another
has to give way to a realistic acceptance of differences and
limitations and to the labour of working out, through give
and take, and possibly quarrels and arguments, a practical common way forward. This requires a clear-headed
recognition that a relationship of enduring love is worth
living for and commands priority over everything else.

In finding their way forward, on the one hand the
lovers have to accept each other as they are, not as
they might be in their dreams, and on the other hand
they have to be prepared to change and grow together.
This looks like a contradiction, but it is not. For what
is essential is that both the accepting and the changing
should be done freely, with good will, on the basis of
genuine communication and genuine understanding of
each other. This is not easy. A love which is conditional
on the other changing in a certain way is not love. Often

the affair breaks down in recrimination and bitterness.
But things can go differently. It does often happen that
the lovers have become truly committed to each other
in a way which survives the gradual withdrawal of
projections and comes to express the deeper human
need for self-giving in freedom. It can survive because
it has brought the lovers to know each other well enough
to trust each other and so to overcome the barriers of
fear. I believe we are all born with a propensity to trust
and love others. We love because God first loved us. But
the great enemy of love is fear. Fear creates the defences
which prevent us from giving ourselves. And the defences
lead to disillusionment and rancour which drain away the
crucial goodwill.

Sometimes people settle down to a limited sort of
marriage in which they each lead fairly separate lives,
with very restricted communication about their deeper
feelings and motivations. This may be convenient and
acceptable for some years, but once the wind blows hard
– when one of the partners is tempted to fall in love
with someone else, or one of them faces redundancy,
or the children grow up and leave home, or whatever –
the foundations of the marriage are too shallow to hold.
There is too much fear and resentment, too little love and
goodwill.

Yet a crisis of this sort can also be an opportunity
for the partners to open up communication with one
another, to understand themselves and each other at a
deeper level, and to make a new start with a relationship
that can be far more fruitful and far more precious than
the one they had before. The key to such a process of
healing and growth is to recognize that what we bring
to a marriage – or any other relationship that goes deep
– is ourselves. The obstacles that we encounter to growth
in the relationship are in fact our own hang-ups, our own
sin and sickness (in the sense discussed in Chapter Four).
It is only by understanding our own individual problems
and trying to grow beyond them that we can hope to deal

with the problems of our marriage and bring that into
new growth.

The way *not* to approach these problems is to project
the blame for everything that has gone wrong on to our
partner. There is always a temptation to do this, because
it is the easiest way to exonerate ourselves from blame
and so, more important, to avoid looking deeply and critically into our own nature. We are almost always afraid
of doing this because, deep down, we lack confidence that
we are of any real worth. The *right* way to approach these
problems is to realize that the loving mutual commitment
of marriage (or of a comparable relationship such as that
between a parent and a grown-up child) provides unique
security, and hence a unique healing environment, in
which we can help each other to peel off the layers of
our protective stories, to understand something of the
truth of ourselves, and to grow into truer, freer, more
loving people.

Jim and Elsie had been married for seventeen years
and had two sons of twelve and nine. Jim was a tele-
phone engineer. A routine marriage had gradually
turned into a sour wrangle. Elsie had been to see
her doctor about stress and depression. She felt she
no longer had any respect for Jim and was thinking
of breaking up the marriage. She said he didn't carry
his share of responsibility and didn't listen to her or
answer her explicitly. She was voluble, excitable and
leaned forward in her chair. He was slow, silent and
tended to lean away. He admitted taking 'avoiding
action', but complained she was constantly attacking
him and quickly got excited and angry. When she
nagged him, he tended to react with a silent unblink-
ing stare which carried a load of hostility. Between
them they managed to stifle communication almost
before it started. They had endless quarrels, often
about fairly trivial matters, but both were devoted to
the children and did not want to let them down. Both

had recently started going to Church. Elsie's anger
and criticizing grew out of a sense of humiliation
and very low self-esteem. Her father was dominant
and distant, her mother shy, obedient and unable
or unwilling to give much help or support; her
grandmother was an interfering busybody, and her
younger brother was, she felt, more important to the
family than herself. From the age of one she had
suffered from asthma and all manner of allergies.
Jim, in contrast, had received love and affirmation
from his mother, but his father had died when he
was thirteen, and he had been faced prematurely
with some of the burdens of adult life. He had
developed something of a protective shell and a habit
of avoiding or postponing issues, perhaps with a
subconscious feeling that they might be too much for
him. When he did so, he would retreat and sulk. He
was a skilled engineer and enjoyed his job, but putting his problems into words and analyzing them did
not come easily to him. At this stage the marriage
between Jim and Elsie seemed near to shipwreck,
but fortunately both of them proved ready to work
hard and honestly at improving the situation. This
was partly for the sake of their children, but it was
also relevant that they had become Christians. In
addition money was short; they could hardly afford
to live separately and it is not cynical to suggest that
this probably served as a useful discipline.

The process of trying to rebuild the marriage
took a long time. The first step was to open up
communication, so that each was able to listen to
the other's unmet needs, and to say what there was
about the other's behaviour that was hard to bear
– saying it gently so that the other would be able
to hear. When they had an altercation leading to
vituperation and sulks, much counselling time was
given to analysing what went wrong and reaching –
even though after the event – some sort of agreement

on what had actually happened and how the matter could have been better handled. Elsie was inclined to 'ransack the family cupboard' to bring up incidents which still rankled months and years after they happened, while Jim was inclined to push things under the carpet and try to forget them. Wherever possible an effort was made to sort out each of these issues and reach some resolution, so that it ceased to fester and could be put away into the past.

All this helped them both to understand themselves and each other better. But things did not go smoothly. To begin with, Jim seemed to gain greatly from his new self-understanding, and made considerable efforts to change his behaviour and to show real goodwill to Elsie. She for her part acknowledged that he was genuinely trying, and she made efforts herself, but she found it hard to conjure up much real goodwill or respect for her husband. After six months he became severely depressed as well as angry. He felt they now understood the situation between them much better, but they were just unable to do much about it. He felt defeated and a failure. He said he sometimes hated her. And now it was he who was on the verge of breaking up the marriage. He was urged not to take a major decision while he was in a state of depression, and after about three weeks the depression lifted.

At this stage it was Elsie who was the more firmly convinced that there was too much at stake in the marriage to let it break up. They continued to work at it, and sometimes for weeks on end there was no major disagreement, but every now and then they would slip back into strife and the ground they had gained was lost once more. Elsie went through times of great stress, when she let her anger loose not only on Jim but on the boys, and then felt deeply distressed about the effect this might have on them. When she was unhappy, even though she

wanted love and support, she could not respond to a
physical touch or hug, and Jim had to learn the need
for care and tact on this point. The stress of outside
circumstances – including Elsie's relations with her
mother and problems for Jim over his job – made
things harder. Jim went through a second period of
feeling deeply depressed, defeated and fed up. But
soon after this in a counselling session Elsie spontaneously took Jim's hand and suggested that they
should agree to put out of their minds any question
of divorce or separation. Jim responded warmly, and
this was an important turning point, because it gave
them additional security in carrying on their work.

Learning to understand themselves was a help,
but it was not enough. They needed to grow into
different people, with more genuine concern for
each other, less self-preoccupation, more goodwill
and readiness to affirm each other – more love;
and this indeed seemed to be happening, though
inevitably it took time. Gradually their power to cope
and to support each other increased. They began to
join in facing their problems together, instead of
facing each other and indulging in a useless power
struggle. As time went by, it became clearer that the
most serious problem they had to face as a family
was the fact that, deep down, Elsie was constantly
struggling with depression. As a result of the experiences of her childhood she had very little confidence
in herself, and this showed itself in great stress
and nervousness about what other people might
be thinking of her, especially in larger gatherings.
At the same time, deep down, she was fiercely
resentful of past humiliation and what she saw as
failure by her parents and others to give her the
care, attention, help and opportunities which could
have made all the difference. What she needed was
a gradual building up of her confidence, so that she
could be set free from old and inappropriate patterns

of emotional reaction which all too often tangled up
her attempts to deal with the present. By far the best
means of achieving this was the steady support of a
loving, understanding, forbearing husband whom
she in turn could help, support, appreciate and
love; and they were moving, uncertainly but with
encouraging determination, along this road.

This case helps to show how much hard work and goodwill is needed if a relationship which has once gone sour
is to be renewed in love; but it also shows how immensely
worthwhile the effort is. The process involves healing
and transformation in both the individuals concerned,
but true renewal cannot be achieved otherwise. It is
enormously to the credit of Jim and Elsie that they had
enough courage, humility and sticking power to face their
difficulties and go so far towards healing them.

It is worth adding here that Jung's theory of the
anima and the animus stretches further than I have
so far suggested. The first bearer of the projection for
a man, he says, is always the mother and for a woman
the father. It is partly for this reason that the process
of separation from the mother or the father at puberty
is of such delicacy and importance, and in tribal com-
munities is marked by special rites. The anima/animus
does not always take the positive, idealized form which
we recognize when young people fall in love. It can also
take a negative form, particularly when, instead of being
projected, it 'invades' the personality. As P.W. Martin
has put it:

When the anima seizes upon the inferior, unconscious side of the man's personality, the other aspect
appears. Such invasion usually takes the form of a
peevish mood, a mood in which the man will sulk,
make remarks (or, more accurately, find remarks
making themselves) which are petulant, weak, nag-
ging, 'womanish' in the worst sense of the term . . .

He is at one and the same time angry and miserable, resentful and self-pitying . . .

As with the anima, the animus may and does invade the conscious personality. The effect, while equally characteristic, takes a very different form. Invasion by the animus drives the woman to opinionating . . . The animus-possessed woman will withstand, correct, criticize and argue down any opposing point of view, particularly if put forward by a man . . . In much the same way as a man in the grip of the anima will not admit that he is moody, over-sensitive, a woman possessed by the animus is usually unable – at least at the time – to see that she is opinionating . . . Such women are liable at times to 'animus panics'. There is a sudden breakdown of the masculine attitude, a fearfulness over nothing, a bursting into tears, in vivid contrast to the previous hectoring.[8]

I am cautious and a little reluctant about using the Jungian language of personified archetypes. It would be possible to re-express these ideas in terms of the stories we tell ourselves in the unconscious layers of the anticipating self. Nevertheless it is fair to say that some of the troubles of Jim and Elsie can be quite effectively described and understood in terms of an invading anima and an invading animus battling it out together, making it difficult for the true, whole personalities of the two people concerned to emerge. Jung himself has remarked that it is harder to become aware of the anima/animus within us than of the shadow side of our personality, and that it is correspondingly more difficult to be set free from their domination when they inappropriately take charge of our behaviour.

Obstacles to Loving (2): Unforgiveness

It is significant that the difficulties encountered by Jim and Elsie arose out of personal defence mechanisms similar to those we have considered in relation to the healing of individuals – projection and denial being prominent among them. The healing of a relationship, as we have seen, depends on the healing of the individuals. And always both partners have to be involved. This is partly because we are all flawed or wounded people, we all need healing, and partly because as one partner grows into healing there is always a need for the other to grow too in a complementary way. Even if the trouble is mainly on one side, the other needs to become aware of where the trouble lies and to be in a position to help, not obstruct, the process of healing. It is sadly not unusual for a husband who has lived comfortably for twenty years with a wife devoted to looking after him and the children to be surprised, dismayed and resentful when she begins to develop new interests and new self-confidence as the children move away. To be in health is to be growing and changing; to be stuck in a pattern which once served well enough is to be in deep trouble.

Counsellors are familiar with cases in which one partner comes for help, but the other will not join in. On the one hand these others suggest that it is only their partner who has problems: 'You can go and get your hang-ups sorted out if you wish.' On the other hand they are suspicious and sometimes sarcastic about what is going on, and this leads to further barriers between the two. As a generalization, men seem to be more afraid than women to look into themselves and face their problems, perhaps because they are under greater pressure in adolescence and young manhood to establish the image of a strong, capable, independent, even macho individual, and they are correspondingly more afraid of anything which threatens to shake this image. Colin, however, was a husband who found the courage to come for help with his wife, and to face his own need to grow and change:

Colin was thirty-seven, his wife Norma thirty-two. His father had died when he was a child and he

was close to his mother. Ever since leaving school
he had worked with her in the family business
and financially was doing well. There were some
gaps in his self-confidence because of the relative
narrowness of his experience, but sport – nowadays
chiefly golf – played a major part in his life, and he
still went round with a group of friends, many of
whom he had known since school days. After he and
Norma had been married for four years she became
pregnant. Colin had been keen on the idea of starting
a family and he seemed pleased when this happened.
However when Norma was six months pregnant
she discovered that he was having an affair with
another woman. Not only this, he was behaving in
an unsympathetic and unkind way to his wife, and
his mother was doing the same. Norma was deeply
hurt and went back to her own family in Scotland.

However Colin's affair soon petered out. He went
to Scotland to see Norma and persuaded her to come
back to him. Although she forgave him, she found
she could not put the episode behind her – particularly the unkindness he and his mother had shown
her. He for his part admitted that he was entirely in
the wrong. He maintained that he had never been
really in love with the other woman and he could not
understand what had come over him. He and Norma
now had a baby boy to whom both were devoted. He
wanted her to put the whole episode behind her and
forget it; but this she could not do, partly because she
could not understand what had caused him to start
the affair and she felt she could not trust him till
she did. In counselling it became clear that Colin's
aberration had something to do with the pregnancy.
He had established himself successfully as a young
adult and his marriage had not greatly altered his
way of life; he and Norma still went round with his
group of friends, and as a matter of principle they
used to give each other plenty of freedom. Norma

used to go away for six weeks at a time to see
her mother, (and this was what made it easy for
Colin to begin an affair). The prospect of being a
father however disturbed Colin more than he could
admit to himself. He was worried that the baby's
arrival would change his life, restrict his freedom,
and make it impossible for him to give so much time
to sport. The ideas of some of his friends had been
an unfortunate influence. He admitted he might
unconsciously have been trying to prove to himself
that he could still be a success with women but he
reiterated that he had not been infatuated and the
woman concerned now meant nothing to him.

At a deeper level it seemed that Colin had been
faced with venturing out into maturity and discovering a truer self – the transition discussed
in Chapter Two. He had been frightened of the
prospect and reluctant to give up the security of
his old ways, but it was essential that he should
do so. Norma too was faced with this transition
and she too had been apprehensive about having
the baby. In Scotland she had begun to go to church
again and this was a sign of the rethinking that was
being forced upon her. It was a help to both of them
to see the situation in this light, and Norma began to
feel that she had a better understanding of what had
been going on in Colin. Meanwhile they were both
delighted with their baby, Colin had found that he
could easily get in as much golf as he needed, and he
too began to go to church. It was necessary to talk
through the need and scope for full apology and full
forgiveness, as well as many other aspects of their
lives in which there would have to be some change.
These included the relationships of each with both
mother and mother-in-law – the need, not to cut out
the older generation, but to put their own marital
relationship first. There was also the question of
good friends and bad, and whether perhaps it was

time for Colin to care less about the figure he cut
in the eyes of the gang of his old friends. There was
a need for Norma to recognize the importance of his
job in Colin's life. There was the question of the new
place of religion in their lives and the question of
true values which arose out of it. Not least there was
the question of the absolute nature of marriage vows
and the security and freedom to discover your true
self which a true marriage could afford. The prospect
overall was not one of restriction and giving up old
pleasures (though some things would have to go), but
of new discovery and an expansion of life and love.
Fortunately they had enough humility and courage
to talk frankly about these things. There seemed to
be a real chance that after this disastrous episode
there could now be a new start to the marriage on
a much sounder basis.

This case brings out the importance of apology and
forgiveness. Apology is more than a mere expression of
regret. We can all recognize the irritable exclamation:
'Well I've said I'm sorry, why have you got to go on
about it?' The very tone of voice suggests something
less than whole-hearted contrition, rather a desire to
shove the incident back under the carpet and go back
to the way things were before. But a true apology has
to include not merely regret for what happened, or
taking back what was said, but also, when necessary,
an honest explanation of why the incident occurred, and
an intention to be different in future. Without these it can
be impossible for the recipient to offer real forgiveness;
for real forgiveness always means setting a person free
by accepting that an obligation has been discharged.
    What, then, is this obligation? It is to restore openness
and freedom to the relationship, which by implication
you accept as something important. If, as the ostensible
offender, you don't accept the obligation, you just break
the relationship, or reduce it to a polite shell. If you do

accept the obligation and apologize, you put yourself in some sense in the power of the other, who can accept your apology, but does not have to. If your apology is rejected, you are yourself rejected and humiliated. Your most likely recourse is to anger, which immediately puts up the barriers to further genuine communication.

It is by no means always easy to make a wholehearted apology, since this means going back on something of yourself, agreeing to change, and making yourself vulnerable to the other. It also depends to some extent on the other, since you can only apologize wholeheartedly for what you genuinely regret; and that may or may not be sufficient to appease the other's hurt. If you cannot make your apology strictly honest, that is, if you do not honestly want to change in the way the other seems to require, the apology does not in fact set you free, it merely becomes a new burden to you.

Conversely it is by no means always easy to forgive wholeheartedly. If you doubt the truth of the other's explanations or his or her real resolution to change, and consequently you still feel insecure, it is hard to forgive and it may be unwise to do so. Furthermore, it is possible that you don't really want to set the other free. Consciously or not, you may want to keep a hold over the other to mould his or her behaviour in some way which flatters your own idea of yourself. Alternatively, you may both be genuinely at odds over what is the right way forward, in which case it is far better, after honest discussion, to agree openly to disagree than to offer false or half-hearted apologies or false or half-hearted forgiveness.

The upshot is that a quarrel, disappointment or disagreement may provide an opportunity for ultimately deepening and strengthening a relationship. It can do this if it leads to a deeper exploration of the understandings and motivations of the people concerned, honest explanations, and, where appropriate, wholehearted apologies and wholehearted forgiveness. In that event

each will have taken down some defences, given a fuller
account of himself or herself, become more vulnerable to
the other, and established a situation of deeper mutual
trust. Each will then be more free to be his or her true
self in the relationship. They will not have gone back to
the relationship as it was before, they will have developed
and strengthened it. This applies even where honest
disagreements have been brought out into the open and
new limitations to the further growth of the relationship
have thereby been recognized. But any degree of falsity,
whether in the discussion of what happened, or in the
apologies given or in the forgiveness offered, can only
reduce the value of the relationship, making it more of
a prison than an opportunity for helping each other to be
free. As always it is truth which is the healer, however
hard the process.

Obstacles to Loving (3): Manipulation and Power Play

Winnicott has suggested that 'in individual emotional
development the precursor of the mirror is the mother's
face'. When the mother's care and love are focussed
on the baby, she responds to him, and through her
response the baby begins to discover himself. If she
reflects not the baby but her own mood or the rigidity
of her own defences, and if this happens not occasionally
but continually, the baby ceases to discover himself in a
creative way. He looks at her and the world, but without
self-confidence, trying to adjust himself to her moods, but
not effectively creating an authentic self. 'If the mother's
face is unresponsive, then a mirror is a thing to be looked
at, not looked into.' And the baby may grow up too ready
to look at images of himself – the way of narcissism –
rather than in realizing his own authenticity from his
own roots. Winnicott refers to the distorted images of
the painter Francis Bacon: 'Bacon's faces seem to me to
be far removed from perception of the actual; in looking

at faces he seems to me to be painfully striving towards being seen.' The healing of the mind in psychotherapy,

> ... is a long term giving the patient back what the patient brings ... I like to think that if I do this well enough the patient will find his or her own self, and will be able to exist and to feel real. Feeling real is more than existing; it is finding a way to exist as oneself, and to relate to objects as oneself, and to have a self into which to retreat for relaxation.[9]

These speculative insights of Winnicott's provide us with a way into the difficult subject of authenticity, of the true and the false self, and the part they play in relationships. Every individual has an inner self of personal plans related to inner goals, together with a presentational self consisting of the stories he or she tells other people, and an operational self consisting of operational roles, the things which he or she is committed to do by agreement, implicit or explicit, with other people. All of these are part of the anticipating self and there is a need to ensure some consistency between them if the self is not to fall apart. Much the same analysis can be applied to organizations, which, in turn, have their inner plans, their presentational accounts of themselves, and their contractual commitments, e.g. to employees and to other individuals and organizations.

The essential fabric of human society, which makes it possible for people to live together, consists of a complex of organizations, formal and informal. Each of us has a large number of operational roles within organizations, and every such role creates for us, in varying degrees, an obligation to behave in a certain way in certain circumstances. The obligation is incurred in relation to the holder of the corresponding role in the pair, whether it be our parent or our child, our spouse, fellow worker, boss, employer or tax collector, or the passer-by who is telling us the way to the station. Some such roles and

obligations are freely chosen and accepted, others are
adopted under various forms and degrees of coercion,
including the coercion of needing the money. But once,
as responsible adults, we have accepted particular operational roles, our good faith is committed and we cannot
go back on them without penalty. All this builds up the
hard structure of society, though we must not forget
that it exists within a swirl of communication, which
has a continuous influence on individuals and so on the
decisions they take, both alone and within organizations.
Our presentational roles, the stories we tell to other
people, are part of the swirl of communication; and
presentational stories of this kind − other peoples' as
well as our own − can help to determine both the inner
plans which we adopt and the outer behavioural roles to
which we commit ourselves.

This analysis may help to clear our minds as we come
to the question of the exercise of power in relationships.
Power is a matter of making other people do what you
want. It can be exerted as physical force, or the threat
of it − the power that grows out of the barrel of a
gun. Or it can be exerted as a matter of authority,
deriving from rank and position in an organization.
Or it can be exerted in open persuasion, the attempt
through presentation and argument to change a person's
mind (which means changing his or her inner goals and
plans). Or it can be exerted through covert persuasion,
otherwise manipulation. This can be a conscious device,
when, in effect, we knowingly put on an act to get our
way − the course of the seducer through the ages. Or it
can be a device that we adopt without being aware, or
at least fully aware, of what we are doing. Conscious
manipulation is conscious duplicity, and usually conscious exploitation. But it is not so common as crusaders
against exploitation generally assume, simply because
manipulators nearly always avoid facing up to what they
are doing. Even the indefensible seducer probably tells
himself some story to justify the things he does and so to

hide from the truth. 'Men loved darkness because their
deeds were evil.' Unconscious manipulation, on the other
hand, is exceedingly common; we all have resorted to it
at some time or other. It is the greatest enemy of loving
relationships, because it conceals the truth and replaces
the self-giving of love with exploitation of other people's
weaknesses (or their generosity).

We can most clearly see the whole gamut of these ways
of exerting power in the relationships between parents
and children. Parents have physical power over their children while they are small, and sometimes they exercise
it or threaten it: 'If you don't stop doing that, I'll smack
you'. But children themselves have power from an early
age. When small, to refuse to eat their food, or to throw it
on the floor from the high chair, can be an effective ploy
for putting pressure on their mum. Struggles over going
to bed are familiar events in many families; as also, a few
years further on, are struggles over how late the teenager
is allowed to stay out in the evening. Open persuasion
and argument often play a part in all this. Persuasion
can, more or less legitimately, include bribery in one form
or another ('If you're a good boy, Mummy will take you to
the circus tomorrow'), or blackmail in one form or another
('If you insist on reading sociology, I won't help with your
university fees'). Open persuasion, however, can easily
shade into conscious or unconscious manipulation: 'Your
father would turn in his grave if he thought you were
going to marry a black man'; 'Honestly, teacher, there
isn't a table in the house that I can do my homework
on'. There is the mother-in-law who always becomes ill
and in need of attention just when the family is about
to go on holiday. There is the man who storms or sulks
when he does not get his way. Illness is used for all kinds
of ulterior ends, and by no means always consciously: the
migraine that comes at a most inconvenient moment can
be a very genuine migraine. Parental love can often be
unconsciously controlling and possessive. For their own
unacknowledged reasons parents often do not want to let

go when children begin to grow away from them. Often they are tempted to try to live vicariously through their children, moulding their lives to fulfil ambitions they were not able to achieve themselves.

The fact is that in every continuing human relationship, whether in the family or the office, the golf club or the board room, the trade union or the pub, there is an element of power play. We want the relationship to continue because it is of value to us; but each of us is getting, or wants to get, something different from it; and each of us has different priorities. What is needed, if the relationship is to be free and rewarding to both parties, is for the two, through honest discussion, to reach some agreement on what their joint priorities are, so that they can together face outwards towards their problems, rather than inwards in confrontation with each other. This means compromise, and therefore inevitably some sacrifice by each (though often for great gain); and it is only possible where there is goodwill on both sides, in other words genuine concern for the other's good, and so for the other's priorities as well as one's own. The alternative is a relationship in which people feel constantly under pressure and, for defensive reasons, give away as little as possible. They end up acting a part in the relationship, rather than being freely themselves.

Very often the pressure that is felt is pressure to play up to the stories the other person tells, or wants to have told, about himself or herself; and often we collude in doing this, either knowingly (and grinding our teeth) or unwittingly (and with an undefined dissatisfaction). Examples are the boss in the office, who needs continually to be flattered; or the boss who acts always as prosecuting counsel, interrupting you and twisting your words before you have a chance to explain yourself. Sometimes there is a 'neurotic fit', through which each partner willingly colludes with the other in reinforcing the other's story, and together they come to live more in fantasy than reality, putting pressure in turn on

other people to join in the collusion. Often people find
it difficult, in Transactional Analysis terms, to adopt
and hold the role of the Adult; they put on constantly
the mantle of the authoritarian Parent, forcing the other
into the Child mode; or alternatively the mantle of the
wheedling or irresponsible Child, forcing the other to be
a Parent; and sometimes they switch between the two.
Perhaps less often people will continue relentlessly and
prosily in the mode of the Adult, never feeling free to let
go and have a laugh.

In his well-known book *Games People Play*[10] Eric
Berne has acutely anatomized a whole series of these
games, which he groups under a variety of headings,
including Life Games (e.g. Kick Me; See What You
Made Me Do), Marital Games (e.g. If It Weren't For
You; Look How Hard I've Tried), Party Games (e.g.
Why Don't You – Yes But), Sexual Games (e.g. Let's
You and Him Fight; Kiss Off), Underworld Games (e.g.
Let's Pull a Fast One on Joey), and Consulting Room
Games (e.g. I'm Only Trying to Help You; Wooden Leg).
He even has a category of Good Games – 'one whose social
contribution outweighs the complexity of its motivations,
particularly if the player has come to terms with these
motivations without futility or cynicism' – (e.g. Cavalier,
Homely Sage).

Here I can only leave it to the reader to guess what
these titles stand for or, better, to read Berne's book. The
relevance of his work in our present context is essentially
to illustrate the multifarious complexity of the ways in
which we seek to manipulate each other and so to flatter
our own self-deceptions. Berne analyses each game in
terms of its thesis (what I would call the story that its
lead player tells); its underlying aim; the roles that it
involves for all players; examples of the game drawn from
childhood and from adult life; what he calls its paradigm
(its analysis in Parent-Adult-Child terms); the various
moves of the game; and the advantages, internal and
external, psychological and social, for the sake of which

it is played. In all this we are brought back to our central
thesis that it is only by recognizing and facing the truth
– in Berne's words coming to terms with our motivations
and those of other people without futility or cynicism –
that we can we find healing and freedom.

Rose was married to Bob at seventeen. He was ten
years older than she was and he tended to expect
her to be always at home, under his control, and
at his beck and call. He went out on his own,
playing squash or drinking at a club nearby, but
he was suspicious and watched the clock if she ever
went out. He gave a lot of time to his own family
and frequently compared her, to her disadvantage,
with his mother (now senile and in an old people's
home). At first, as a shy girl and partly because of
her own upbringing, Rose was content to go along
with this. But by the time she was twenty-five, with
two children, she was feeling more resentful at being
taken for granted. She had been advised by a doctor
to come for counselling because she was also having
panic attacks, particularly in crowded places. These
seemed to come when she was feeling overwhelmed
by the combination of her husband's expectations,
the work involved in job, home and children, and the
stress of maintaining, in spite of others' disapproval,
her own ambitions to get more qualifications and
find some better employment. The panic attacks
had shaken her growing self-confidence. Who was
she? Fundamentally it seemed that she was a person
growing into her own reality, recognizing her own
capacities and becoming more aware of the way in
which her own development was being frustrated.
The panic attacks reflected the instinctive fear of
the Child within her of what might happen if she
asserted herself in the face of Bob's disapproval (and
also to some extent her father's). When these issues
were brought out into the open, however, and she

began to understand better the roots of Bob's behaviour, her confidence returned. Bob had always been desperate to please his mother, but she had never given him much love. In his insecurity he had a great need to keep things under control, and he had tended to keep his young wife in the Child mode (or ego state as Berne would put it), while he took refuge in an authoritarian, judging Parent mode. As she grew in confidence and maturity, she could no longer happily collude in this pattern of behaviour. She was now an Adult at least as strong and able as he was, and at some point there would have to be a crunch. Rose had no intention of breaking up the marriage and the best hope for the future lay in Bob's accepting her growing maturity, while himself being ready to adopt an Adult mode in sharing responsibility with her, rather than trying to keep himself in a separate, controlling position.

I do not know what eventually happened in this situation. There was bound to be a confrontation, and this could have one of three possible outcomes. Bob might stick rigidly to his position, while Rose stood out for her own independence: in due course the marriage would break up. Or Bob might prevail and Rose might knuckle under. Or both might show real readiness to listen to each other and talk their problems through, with the result that both would grow in freedom and confidence, and the marriage would be far more strongly established than ever before. In other words there could be anger and tears leading either to parting, or to bitter submission, or to growth in love and true personal authenticity.

Anger, Tears and Reconciliation

Anger is the emotion we feel when we are frustrated. In a relationship it can flare up when we cannot get what we want, or when we feel ourselves forced into a false position. When we are angry we stop listening, we turn instead to the idea of using force. Our sense of reality or self-preservation may keep us from physical violence, but we may nevertheless shout at the other and say everything possible to hurt. The other may well reply in kind, and often the relationship will be brought to an end, or at least reduced to a superficial formality.

Tears by contrast reflect pain. In an argument they can mark the surrender of one party, but surrender in a fashion which makes a strong claim for sympathy; they may perhaps help to melt the other's heart and so bring the other round to a bit of surrender too. Both anger and tears, when they are genuine, reflect a breaking through of the authentic person, the deeper feelings and motivations which underlie the social act that people are putting on. To that extent they may be helpful in establishing a new basis of reality on which the relationship can be rebuilt in a new and sounder way. But anger in particular achieves this only through the destruction of what was there before; and sometimes rebuilding may not be possible. Tears may seem a better basis for reconciliation, but we need to be cautious. Tears, especially perhaps in women, can easily become a refuge from anger. If you have grown up with a feeling that anger is always bad, and if you have little self-esteem anyway, it may be difficult to acknowledge or express your anger, and all too easy to dissolve in tears instead. When that happens truth is not served and no true foundation is being laid for reconciliation.

We are imperfect humans and at best we achieve loving relationships only imperfectly, partially, and with some people more than with others. Even in the most perfect marriage each partner will have some areas of privacy or holding back, which the other will have the sensitivity to respect. But what of the cases where the reciprocal process of understanding and trust does not work? It may be that we cannot overcome our own pride or defensiveness, or the other puts expectations

on us that we cannot truthfully accept, or betrays our
trust, or demands affirmations from us which we cannot
truthfully give. Such cases run from the otherwise good
relationship which has an awkward no-go area to the
marriage which is an empty shell, with two partners
barely speaking to each other, or again to a relationship
of mutual torment and recrimination (as for example in
Who's afraid of Virginia Woolf?), or to one of virtual
domination or enslavement by one partner of the other.

Every such relationship is different from every other in
complex ways. But we are all involved in relationships,
and in the real world difficulties are inescapable, failure
is always around. What should we do about situations
of failure? The first rule must clearly be to refrain from
blaming. Judgment in the sense of condemnation is for
God, not us (and God is merciful). Blaming merely helps
us to build up new defences ourselves and, by provoking
resentment, helps the other to do the same. The second
rule must be to remain as humble and clear-eyed as
possible. We are all 'poor bloody humans'. On this basis
we can try to establish certain boundaries, identifying on
each side the self-image which has to be respected, the
point beyond which you do not interfere, whatever your
own opinion may be. The result is a relationship which
is more restricted than ideally it could be, but one which
enables the maximum of communication to continue.

The more we can keep the channels of communication
open, the more the healing power of truth will be able to
do its work. But in such cases the condition of keeping
the channels open is restraint. Our aim may be to help
others to achieve truth about themselves; but the last
way to do this, in most circumstances, is to tell them
exactly what we think is wrong with them. Whatever
we say, it will only be our opinion. It may be correct,
but if we deliver it in 'blunt Yorkshireman' fashion it
will seem like a threat. When people pride themselves
on their frankness, there is often an aggressive will to
hurt or dominate behind their words, which is concealed

from their consciousness but is not so easily concealed
from others. We have continually to be sensitive to where
the other is and what the other can stand, as well as
continually aware of where we are ourselves and what
our own deeper motivations may be. We need to have
respect and care for the other and never to lose that
good will which is God's will. This is the course of the
suffering servant. It is much easier, and gets rid of some
of the pain, to lash out in anger, to deliver 'home truths',
to blame and condemn, to justify oneself, to feel contempt,
to keep a cold distance, to take a hard line, – finally to
break off or freeze the relationship. But this does not
serve the truth.

> Set a guard, Lord, upon our tongues;
> that we may never speak
> the cruel word which is not true,
> or, being true, is not the whole truth,
> or, being wholly true, is merciless;
> for the love of Jesus Christ our Lord.[11]

There is of course a place for angry self-assertion in a
relationship, provided it is spontaneous, unselfconscious
and hot-blooded. The very explosion can be therapeutic.
It can make a person finally aware of a truth about
himself or someone else which he would otherwise have
avoided facing. It can induce a new respect and lead to a
deeper reconciliation. It can sharply mark a boundary to
attempted manipulation or domination or possessiveness
– but it must not be allowed to persist. As St Paul said,
'be angry, and sin not: let not the sun go down upon
your wrath'.[12] To approve our own anger while we are
being angry is already a bit sick. To cultivate a cold,
conscious, long-term anger (as distinct from a quiet
determination), even in what we believe is a good cause,
is to cultivate hatred. We use anger to defend ourselves
against encroachment, and its most constructive use may
be to establish the boundaries which are needed in an

imperfect relationship. But once the boundaries have been set and accepted, and a *modus vivendi* has been found, anger is no longer needed. Further communication can then be developed, and we can hope that eventually more trust will grow and it may become possible to lower some of the defences. But the process cannot be rushed.[13]

The course of the suffering servant, the follower of Christ, does not mean that we should accept domination or collude with manipulation, as we may well be tempted to do. But it may sometimes require us, while not deceiving ourselves about what is happening, to put up with an unsatisfactory relationship rather than break it altogether. Here a deep discernment may be required – first of our own motives, for if we collude out of weakness or fear, this can never serve the truth; secondly of the motives of the other; and thirdly of the consequences in the longer-term of what we do. We may have to choose between evils, as often in this world. The criterion of choice is: what will eventually bring the most truth, the most love, the least hate into the situation? That criterion is not easy to apply; but then, life is not easy to live.

NOTES

Introduction
1 D.W. Winnicott, Introduction to *Therapeutic Consultations in Child Psychiatry*, quoted in Adam Philips, *Winnicott* (London, Fontana, 1988) p. 143.
2 D.W. Winnicott, *Playing and Reality* (London, Penguin, 1974) p. 102.

Chapter One   I Want to be Me: Childhood and Adolescence

1 It is in this sense that I would understand the doctrine of St Thomas Aquinas (and Aristotle) that the soul is the form of the body.
2 1 Corinthians 15:42–44
3 Romans 7:15 REB.
4 Shakespeare, *Hamlet*, Act 1, Sc. 3.
5 Erik H. Erikson, *Childhood and Society*, 2nd. Edition 1963 (London, Triad/Paladin Paperbacks, 1977).
6 R.D. Laing, *The Divided Self*, (London, Penguin, 1965).
7 Frank Lake, *Clinical Theology*, 1966, Abridged Version (London, Darton, Longman and Todd, 1986).
8 D.W. Winnicott, *Playing and Reality*, *op. cit.* p. 47 and *passim*.
9 Michael Jacobs, *The Presenting Past* (London, Harper and Row, 1986) p.61.
10 See Eric Berne, *Games People Play*, (London, Penguin, 1968).

Chapter Two   I Want to be Me: The Adult World

1 Erik H. Erikson, *op. cit.* p. 237.
2 I think the quotation comes from William James, *The Varieties of Religious Experience* 1902, but I have not been able to locate it exactly.
3 C.G. Jung, *Modern Man in Search of a Soul*, (London, Kegan Paul, 1933) p. 264.
4 C.G. Jung, *Psychological Types* (London, Kegan Paul, Trench, Trubner, 1946).
5 C.G. Jung, *The Secret of the Golden Flower*, quoted in Fordham, *An Introduction to Jung's Psychology* (London, Penguin, 1953).
6 John 3:3, 7–8 REB.
7 Romans 6:3, 6, 14 REB.
8 Ephesians 4:12–13 REB.
9 T.S. Eliot, 'Little Gidding' from *Four Quartets* (London, Faber and Faber, 1944).
10 T.S. Eliot, 'East Coker' from *Four Quartets*, *op. cit.*
11 Ibid.
12 I have found Colin Murray Parkes, *Bereavement* (London, Tavistock, 1972) particularly helpful.

Chapter Three   Stories to Tell

1 A much fuller account of the ideas briefly sketched in these paragraphs is given in Edward Moss, *Seeing Man Whole: A New Model for Psychology* (The Book Guild, Lewes, 1989). (This book is now out of print; copies are available from the author at 29 Guildown Avenue, Guildford GU2 5HA.)
2 The map is of a flexible, quasi-topological kind. That is to say, angles, distances and areas are indefinitely flexible, the scale can be vast or minute, yet neighbourhood, sequence and consequently *relative* location on the map as projected from Me-Here-Now can still be identified. The situation located can then be brought to a focus, at the appropriate scale, in an *image*, vague or precise.

3 S. Freud, *New Introductory Lectures* (London, Hogarth Press, 1933) p.98.

4 See Edward Moss *op. cit.* for a more detailed account. In respect of the theory of systems and information I have relied on W. Ross Ashby, *An Introduction to Cybernetics* (London, Chapman & Hall, 1956) and *Design for a Brain* (Chapman & Hall, Revised Edition, 1960); and on James G. Miller, *Living Systems* (McGraw-Hill, 1979).

5 See *The Magical Number Seven* in G.A. Miller, *The Psychology of Communication*, (London, Penguin, 1968). In a wider perspective Michael Polanyi's theory of tacit knowing offers some profound insights into the multi-levelled complexity of human thought and perception. See in particular Michael Polanyi, *Personal Knowledge* (London, Routledge and Kegan Paul, corrected edition 1962); and Michael Polanyi, *Knowing and Being* (London, Routledge and Kegan Paul, 1969).

6 John 8:31, 32, 37, 43–47 RSV.

7 John 14:6 RSV.

8. John 3:6–8 RSV.

9 John 3:16 RSV.

10 John 3:19–21 RSV.

11 John 9:39, 41 RSV.

Chapter Four   I Want to be Free

1 St. Augustine, *Contra adversarium legis et prophetarum*, I 4 f, quoted by C.G. Jung in *Aion*, 1951.

2 Romans 8:20–23 REB.

3 1 Corinthians 15:26 AV.

4 Job 42:3–5 REB.

5 See John Polkinghorne, *Science and Creation* (London, SPCK, 1988) and *Science and Providence* (London, SPCK, 1989).

6 C.G. Jung, *Aion*, Collected Works Vol. 9, Pt. II, p.53.

7 Ibid, pp.216–217.

8 Jung favours a Quaternity not least because it lends

itself to symmetrical symbolic representation as a
'mandala'. But the identity of the fourth member of
the Quaternity seems to vary somewhat according to
the context. Sometimes he implies that it is the Virgin
Mary. While the Trinity encompasses the good, the
spiritual and the masculine, it fails in his view to
include the material, the feminine and the evil. Satan
is required as a member in order to balance Christ
as one of the 'Hostile Brothers' of the zodiacal Age
of Pisces; but he would seem to have a multiple role
if all three of these elements are to be brought into
the Quaternity. See e.g. 'A Psychological Approach to
the Dogma of the Trinity' (CW para. 252) in *Psychology and Western Religion*, (London, Ark Paperback
edition, 1988) p.67. (Jung incidentally, in suggesting
that the material is excluded from the Trinity shows a
fundamental misunderstanding of the theology of the
incarnation.)

9 He does turn to love in the last paragraph (excluding
the brief 'Retrospect') of his *Memories, Dreams,
Reflections*, 1963 (London Fontana Edition, 1967).
But, apart from quoting some phrases from St Paul,
he can only say repeatedly in different ways that there
is nothing he can say.

10 From her comments in *The Independent* on a series
of articles in that newspaper on her book *Celebration* (London, Fount, 1989). On the God who suffers
see also W.H. Vanstone, *Love's Endeavour Love's
Expense* (London, Darton, Longman and Todd, 1977).

11 Matthew 5:48 AV.

12 John Rawls, *A Theory of Justice* (Oxford, 1972).

13 Carl Rogers, *Carl Rogers on Personal Power* (London,
Constable, 1978).

14 Jonathan Sacks, *The Persistence of Faith* (Reith
Lectures, 1990), (London, Weidenfeld and Nicolson,
1991) pp. 41–2.

15 John 10:10 AV.

16 Luke 9:24 AV.

17 John 8:36 RSV.

18 Galatians 5:1 RSV.

19 Romans 8:21 RSV.

20 James 1:15 RSV.

21 2 Corinthians 5:4 RSV.

22 John 3:14–15 RSV. Romans 11:32.

23 Romans 3:24 RSV.

24 2 Corinthians 3:7 AV.

25 Romans 8:2 NIV.

26 Romans 11:32 RSV.

27 Romans 2:14, 15 RSV.

28 T.S. Eliot, 'Little Gidding', *op. cit.*

29 Gerald G. May M.D. *Addiction and Grace* (London, Harper and Row, 1988) p.9.

30 There has recently been a remarkable revival of interest in the use of the 'Spiritual Exercises' of St Ignatius, based upon relatively prolonged periods of silent retreat (eight days or thirty days), during which retreatants have daily interviews with their directors and focus their prayer on passages from the Bible, individually selected in relation to their own situations and the healing 'process of Christ'.

31 Oliver W. Sacks, *Awakenings*, Revised Edition (Penguin, 1976).

32 C.S. Lewis, *A Grief Observed* (London, Faber and Faber Ltd., 1961).

33 Oliver W. Sacks, *Awakenings*, *op. cit.* p.314n.

34 Ibid, pp.293–4, 297, 301–2.

35 Ibid, pp.315–6.

36 The nature of depression and how to treat it are matters of some controversy. Dorothy Rowe has written extensively on depression, denouncing those who regard it as basically a physical disease to be treated by drugs (my reference is particularly to her recent comprehensive book *The Depression Handbook*, London, Collins, 1991). I have reservations about some of her more sweeping statements and I

do not share all her attitudes, but essentially I believe her approach to depression is sound. I would wish to combine it however with some of the ideas of Dr. May and to place it within the theoretical framework sketched in this book, and described more fully in my *Seeing Man Whole*.

37 John 3:17–18 RSV.
38 Julian of Norwich and, in his later works, William Law are among the writers who have taken a similar view. See also Robert Llewelyn, *With Pity Not With Blame* and *Love Bade Me Welcome*; and Robert Llewelyn and Edward Moss, *Fire from a Flint*: *Daily Readings with William Law* (all Darton, Longman and Todd, 1982, 1985 and 1986 respectively).
39 1 John 4:18 RSV. The Authorized Version uses the accurately descriptive phrase 'fear hath torment'.
40 1 Corinthians 15:48–49 RSV.

Chapter Five Loving and Being Loved

1 Erving Goffman, *The Presentation of the Self in Everyday Life*, (Penguin 1971), Introduction.
2 Ibid. Introduction.
3 See Erving Goffman, *Relations in Public* (Penguin 1972); see also Erving Goffman, *Encounters*, and *Interaction Ritual*, (both published in the UK by Penguin in 1972).
4 Anthony Storr, *The Integrity of the Personality*, 1960 (Penguin Edition, 1963) p.91.
5 Ibid, p.106.
6 P.W. Martin, *Experiment in Depth* (London, Routledge and Kegan Paul, 1955) p.81.
7 Anthony Storr *op. cit.* pp.123–124.
8 P.W. Martin, *op. cit.* pp.82–87.
9 D.W. Winnicott, *op. cit. Playing and Reality* p.134.
10 Eric Berne, *op. cit.*
11 I have not been able to identify the origin of this prayer.

12 Ephesians 4:26 AV.
13 Alastair V. Campbell, *The Gospel of Anger* (London, SPCK, 1986) is an interesting and wide-ranging study, though in my judgment Campbell leans over a little too much in favour of anger. It is also worth mentioning Bacon's shrewd and epigrammatic essay 'Of Anger'. As Bacon says, 'The Scripture exhorteth us *To possess our souls in patience*. Whosoever is out of patience is out of possession of his soul. Men must not be like bees, that put their lives in the sting.'

Name and Subject Index

Note: To provide the equivalent of a glossary, technical terms and words given a special meaning in the text are italicized in the index; in these cases page numbers indicating where explanations or definitions of the terms concerned may be found are printed in bold type.